not on fiche. ✗

RELIGION
AND
LIFE

ARNOLD RADEMACHER

RELIGION
AND
LIFE

SCEPTER

CHICAGO—DUBLIN—LONDON

ORIGINAL TITLE IN THE GERMAN:
RELIGION UND LEBEN
(VERLAG HERDER K.G., FREIBURG)

First published 1961

CONTENTS

Preface
to the first edition

Now that we are living in an era very different, in many ways, from any that went before it, and which will determine the destinies of future generations for years to come, every Christian who lives through these fateful years has an obligation to help in preparing the way for the birth of a 'new man' and for the establishment of a truly Christian culture. For some time now, this thought has moved us to call for an increased awareness of this crisis and to awaken the feeling among men of their responsibility to work for a favourable solution. We have spoken on this subject in lectures before numerous academic gatherings, especially at a convention of the Catholic Academic Federation at Dresden and in lectures to students of all Faculties at the University of Bonn. All the individual crises of our times can ultimately be traced to the separation which exists between religion and life, between Christianity and humanism, between Catholicism and profane culture. Hence a reunion between these elements is at once a prerequisite for, and a key to, the solution of all modern humanity's problems.

There have always been two possible, and indeed essential, ways of achieving unity between religion and life. In this book we are going to discuss and recommend one of them in particular: that is, the way of what we shall call the religious activist. We have decided to deal with this way, firstly, because up to now it has received very little theological treatment, while the other way, that of the mystic who lives removed from the world, has already been abundantly studied. Another reason for the importance of this way is that the enormous strides which have lately been made in the external domination of nature demand all the more urgently the infusion of a 'soul' and spiritual values into this cultural activity. In our discussion of this form of life the reader will find, we venture to hope, the basic principles of an asceticism applicable to a life in the world; and it seems to us most urgent that our present-day theology should build further on these principles.

Arnold Rademacher

Preface
to the second edition

This book has attracted widespread attention and has been made the subject of numerous lectures and discussions in various societies and circles. This seems to us a fair indication that the ideas which it contains, and for which it tries to awaken an understanding, are in tune with the times. Only a few critics have found our picture of the contemporary religious and cultural situation too gloomy.

It is true that there may be a big difference between seeing the situation in a theoretical way and feeling personally involved in it to the extent of trying to bring about some reform. But if the false optimism shown in glittering judgements of our times has been shaken, and if the true optimism which comes only from faith has received some encouragement, then this book will not have been written in vain.

In this edition, we have made use of many suggestions, especially concerning the relation between activity and contemplation, made to us and for which we are very grateful.

Arnold Rademacher

1

The relationship
between religion and life

UNITY IN NATURE AND IN THE SPIRITUAL LIFE

Unity is a fundamental and essential factor in man and in nature. All our thinking and striving is directed towards unity: unity of thought, a unified conception of the world, unity of character and of moral personality. Unity in itself is a perfection, something good, a real value; and the more profound philosophies have always either taken great pains to demonstrate this or else have laid great stress on it as an *a priori* axiom. For the neo-platonics, God, the highest and most perfect Being, is the *One*. Theologians tell us that in God there is no distinction between essence and existence, between nature and person, between potency and act, between substance and accident. Multiplicity, on the other hand, is in itself a privation, an evil. Now, unity takes various forms in different spheres: in the universe it is the cosmos; in organic life, it is health; in logical thinking, it is knowledge; in social and political life, it is prosperity and peace. In these spheres multiplicity, that is to say, lack of unity, takes the form of chaos, sickness, error, sin, death and war. Multiplicity, however, can take on some meaning and value when many elements are joined to form some superior unity. In that case harmony is, in itself, beautiful with a beauty which is the reflection of order. A mixture of colours, for instance, is formed into a superior unity by the idea behind the picture; a chaotic jumble of signs becomes a unity by virtue of the meaning of the whole piece of writing; a mass of individual men are welded into the superior unity of a society by the fact of some common purpose. Unity and harmony are a criterion of truth, a sign of order, a condition for strength and a guarantee of permanency.

Unity in nature

The first and most self-evident unity which presents itself to us is the unity of the universe.[1] The universe is a cosmos. And this holds good in spite of occasional elements which seem to be in disorder or at variance with their purpose in the scheme of things. In fact, often when these apparent elements of disorder and contradiction are seen from a higher point of view and with more detailed knowledge, it becomes evident that even they proceed from the law and harmony which rule the universe. Nature is governed by the law of continuity, that is to say, all its parts are perfectly fitted one to another, leaving no 'empty' spaces, no vacuum. *Natura non facit saltus*, was the way the ancients expressed it. Leibnitz also formulated a law of continuity, which stated that there are no gaps in nature and that all its parts flow over one into another by a process of imperceptible transition. This unity of nature is not a mere mechanical unity, a mere juxtaposition of the parts, but rather a dynamic unity, the result of the interaction of forces of attraction and repulsion which are in a state of constant tension with one another. A removal of this tension would lead to death and the destruction of the world.

The principles of order in nature are called, generally speaking, the laws of nature. In the case of man, for instance, the principle of biological unity is the sexual instinct; the principle of sociological unity is the social instinct; the principle of cultural unity is speech; the principle of religious unity is man's natural tendency to worship a supreme Being.

In so far as he is a part of nature, man also forms a unity in himself, in his relationship to the things of the world around him and in his relationship to God. There is a harmonious relation of unity between his body and his soul; and this unity is not a mere external, moral, artificial union, as if the soul were imprisoned in the body to punish a guilt incurred by it before its union with the body, as Plato would hold;

[1] Cf. Hans André, *Die Einheit der Natur:* an essay in biography and natural philosophy, Habelschwerdt 1923 ; and by the same author, *Welteinheit als Grundgedanke der neuen Kosmologie*, in Hochland XXII, April 1925, pp. 95–103.

nor as a transition stage to a future state of pure spirituality, as many theosophists would say; but rather they unite to form a whole, an intrinsic, physical and essential unity with new and specific ends, potencies and activities. There is a unity also between the various faculties of the soul. We may separate these faculties for the purpose of studying them more closely, but all the while we realise that this separation is artificial, and that in reality, these faculties are closely united and bound up with one another. There is also a unity between man and nature. In so far as he is a material being, man is subject to the same laws as the natural world which surrounds him. He is part of the course of the world and of nature and he shares in the destiny of the cosmos. But he also has a responsibility towards the world of nature and is called to cooperate in the propagation and the completion of nature.

The same also holds true in the order of salvation. St. Paul says that all nature groans and travails in pain awaiting the revelation of the sons of God.[2] He sees all of creation in one grandiose unity, when he says: 'For all is yours, and you are Christ's, and Christ is God's.'[3]

There is also a unity between man and man, and between man and society. Men are not just atoms floating around in space, only occasionally and fleetingly meeting each other. They are the cells of an organism, in which each cell serves the whole and the whole serves each cell; they are bound together in a community of life and work and share a common destiny. There is also a unity between man and God. From the point of view of the submission of man to God, this unity is called religion, while from the point of view of God's communicating himself to man, it is grace, revelation, beatification. No profound system of philosophy or theology can feel satisfied with the cold relationship set up by Deism between God and man.

Unity in the spiritual life

Man's relationship with other creatures is governed not only by that intrinsic necessity which makes him part of creation: in addition, since he is a moral being, he can and has an obligation to create unity and to further the degree of unity which already exists, by shaping the raw material of the world

[2] Romans, 8, 22 ff; [3] 1 Corinthians, 3, 23.

into a harmonious unity, which will bear his own image and
the image of God. But whereas other living creatures, inanimate
things being governed by the forces of nature and living
creatures by their instincts, must naturally tend towards this
unity by virtue of the immanent laws which govern them,
man alone, by virtue of his freedom, can violate and even
destroy this unity. He can cause discords in nature and can
place himself and all of nature in a state of rebellion against
God. He can help to complete the work of creation by perfecting the world, but he can also ally himself with godless
and destructive elements. He can cause division and friction
between body and soul, between nature and culture, man and
man, people and people, class and class, city and country,
man and woman, the world and God.

For man, unity is a duty; he must create harmony and make
himself the mouthpiece of the mute praise offered to God by
inanimate and brute creation. In the matter of knowledge as
in love, man is drawn irresistibly to seek unity. He feels the
urge to reduce the complexity and multiplicity of natural
phenomena to a unified and harmonious concept of the world.
And since knowledge is nothing more than the reduction of the
multiple to a unity in relation to some principle of cause,
every man may be said in this sense to be a philosopher.
Every thinker aspires to a philosophical conception of the world
which will unify all its various aspects. Kant says that to derive
everything from one principle is 'the inexorable need of human
reason, which can find full satisfaction only in a perfect and
systematic unification of all its knowledge.'[4] Humanity has
always aspired to the construction of an organic science, the
philosophia perennis, and to the realisation of the unity between
religion and the Church. Parallel to this desire is the striving
of our better nature after a unified, well-developed personality.
There is no man who does not wish for this unity and harmony
of character and personality, who would not wish to be, as it
were, poured from a single mould.

In men of every era and culture we find this intense longing
for repose within a unity of life. This is an echo of that harmonious unity which existed formerly in Paradise and which
will one day in the future be realised in heaven; a dream of a
state of blessed peace, in which nature is subject to man, the
body to the soul and the soul to God. We see this longing in

[4] *Kritik der praktischen Vernunft* I 1 3, edited by Karl Kehrbach
at Leipzig, p. 110.

Ovid's prophetic descriptions of a Golden Age, in which every man will practise loyalty and justice without any need for the sanctions of law, where there will be no written laws and no sin, no judge and no punishment. We see it in the hopes of Imperial Rome for a future millenium under a divine ruler, as described by Virgil in the fourth Eclogue. We see it in the descriptions by the prophets of a time of everlasting peace to come, when the swords will be turned into ploughshares and the lances into sickles,[5] when the wolf will lie with the lamb and the panther with the doe, when the calf and the lion will feed together and a child shall lead them, when the cow and the she-bear will feed together and their young ones rest together, when the lion will eat straw like the ox, when the suckling child shall play where the asp lies and the weaned child shall lay his hand on the basilisk, and the earth shall be filled with the knowledge of the Lord, as the covering waters of the sea,[6] where every man shall sit under his vine or under his fig tree and there shall be none to make them afraid.[7]

We also find the same dream in the description of the millenium in the Apocalypse of St. John. In times of great calamities, especially, this longing inherent in man can rise to a pitch of ecstatic vehemence, and even the most sober and level-headed of thinkers have been brought under its captivating spell. St. Augustine's 'City of God' harmonises all human relations into a divine kingdom, and Kant's 'Ethical state upon earth', which will be governed by the moral law, are other manifestations of this human longing for repose and unity carried over into the religious and moral spheres. And when we come to examine carefully Karl Marx's future state and even the present Soviet system, we see that at the root of both of them lies this same nostalgia for a visible Paradise. The Indian prophet-poet Tagore, in his drama 'The King of the dark chambers',—the King being God—gives us a glimpse of such a kingdom with its beatific harmony.

THE LAW OF TENSION

When we compare these longings of which we have been speaking with the actual reality, we find a very different picture. There has never been a time in history when this

---

[5] Isaias, 2, 4; [6] Isaias 11, 6–9; [7] Micheas 4, 3.

idea of unity, repose and harmony has been realised. And yet we can never entirely abandon hope of its ultimate fulfilment. We are faced, then, with a conflict between things as they are and things as they ought to be and as we hope they will be one day. To restore unity is a duty imposed on man: an ideal goal which stretches into infinity.

But no straight path leads to this unity; it is achieved by a union of opposites. Opposites are brought together, a state of tension is set up between them, and this tension discharges itself in the form of energy to be followed by further tensions and further discharges. In this constant interaction between opposing forces we have a vital law of nature and humanity. This continual disturbance of the balance resulting from the opposing tensions brings out the latent energies of men and of things and puts them to work for the advancement of progress in their particular spheres. This law of tension, therefore, is a principle of conservation and of progress; and it is so important for a deeper understanding of the basic relationship between religion and life that it will be worth our while to examine the whole concept of tension more closely.

What is tension?

The concept of tension is taken from the science of mechanics, where it is used to indicate the mutual action of forces. The essential prerequisite for a state of tension is that the forces in question must be mutually opposed and yet be related or of the same kind. The opposition, therefore, is not one of hostility, but one of polarity.

Tensions may be mechanical, electric or chemical. Thus, for instance, a tension is set up between two poles which are charged with positive and negative electricity. In a mechanical tension, the element of relationship consists in the fact that the two forces are of the same order, while the element of opposition is brought about by the fact that the two forces are straining in opposite directions, just as when an elastic band is stretched. However, tension in itself is a state of equilibrium; it is not yet an active force. But it is potential energy, in the sense that it is capable of producing work. When the state of equilibrium is destroyed this potential energy, which is latent in the state of tension, is converted into the energy of motion or kinetic energy. The change from potential into kinetic energy produces work and thereby heightens the value of the forces which are concerned in this state of tension. However, if this work is to have any duration there must be a constant repetition of this transformation from potential into kinetic energy. The light of an electric bulb, for instance, is the result of a continuous oscillatory discharge.

Now all other things being equal, the greater the distance between the positive and the negative poles, the greater will be the tension generated between them; thus, the greater the distance between the positive and negative poles of an electric conductor, the greater the electrical tension generated. The more taut the bowstring, the further it will shoot the arrow. Tension produces work; the greater the tension, the greater the discharge of energy, and the greater the discharge of energy the greater the work done. If after each discharge of energy no new source of energy comes along, there can be no further work done. When the tension between the forces reaches a certain pitch, the forces cannot sustain it any longer, the equilibrium between them is destroyed and there is a discharge of energy. This process is very well illustrated in the act of walking. The first step taken from a standing position makes the body tend to fall, hence it destroys the stability or equilibrium of the body. If the body is restored to a position of equilibrium, then it is brought to a standstill; but if the counter-movement taken to restore stability goes beyond that which is needed to re-establish equilibrium, as happens when the body takes a further step, then there is a further disruption of equilibrium, which calls for yet another movement. Hence the process of walking consists of a series of tensions and loss of equilibrium, with resultant discharges of energy, due to the instability brought about by the successive steps.

If the opposing forces are to produce work or activity, then they must be brought together in a state of reciprocal tension. If this tension is removed, the two forces are cut apart and there is nothing to bring them into relation with one another. There is, as it were, a rupture or chasm between them, which rules out any interaction or intercommunication between them to produce work or energy. This rupture, then, is a principle of sterility, and it is only when it is somehow bridged that a new tension can be set up and the two forces brought once more into fruitful relationship. The two forces in tension are mutually orientated towards each other, and strive to arrive at a state of equilibrium, to construct a parallelogram of forces. If one force disappears, then the other one is powerless to function. If one end of the bowstring is untied, then the other end, no matter how tightly tied, is powerless and the bow cannot fire an arrow; it is only when both ends of the bowstring are tightly secured that the bow has the power to shoot an arrow.

In the intellectual sphere, there is a state of tension when knowledge and ignorance concerning the same object coexist side by side, or when two opinions on the same object come into conflict. In the former case, the relation is one of *aporia*, or uncertainty, while in the second it is *antinomia*, or opposition. Both provoke an investigation which will restore the equilibrium between knowledge and ignorance or between two opposing views; and this constitutes the point of departure for all philosophical knowledge. When, however, opposition becomes contradiction, then tension ceases and knowledge becomes impossible. In the case of intellectual tension, the common element binding the two poles, or the fulcrum, as it were, through which the tension between them communicates itself, is the desire for knowledge, which is at once fulfilled and unfulfilled. The succession of new problems, new knowledge and again new problems, effects the progress of knowledge, and to this progress there can be no limits. When the desire for knowledge fades, whether through intellectual inertia or through a complacent satisfaction with what has already been achieved, then the fulcrum which joins the two poles and makes them act upon one another is gone, and the progress of knowledge comes to a standstill.

The action of the bodily and intellectual powers are a source of joy and pleasure to the person in whom these powers are vested. Hence the law of tension, by means of which a progressive activity and a continual increase in kinetic energy and efficiency is brought about by the free interplay of forces, constitutes at the same time a principle of happiness. However, an excessive tension between the forces, so excessive that a state of equilibrium cannot be restored, must be guarded against, both in the physical and the intellectual domain; for a destruction of equilibrium without its being restored and releasing a new discharge of energy is equivalent to ruin or standstill, or in the spiritual order to error, sin or despair. Even in the matter of religion, a powerful state of tension can be established between nearness to God and distance from him. The greatest religious tension ever experienced in any soul was that expressed in the cry of the God-man on the Cross: 'My God, my God, why hast thou forsaken me?' But this tension did not dissolve into despair, but was resolved in an expression of infinite trust in the eternal Father: ' Father, into thy hands I commend my spirit.'

A study of the nature of our knowledge reveals that we cannot comprehend the reality which surrounds us except in an imperfect and inadequate way: this is not only because we do not have the time to allow all the elements of reality to pass before our eyes, or because we have not yet acquired the capacity to bring them all within our field or vision, but also because reality is a unity which encompasses us and in which we ourselves are submerged. Hence we can never completely distinguish the knowing subject and the object to be known, or get a completely comprehensive view of reality. There can be no question of a pure subject being face to face with a pure object, since both belong to the one reality, which forms an all-embracing mass, an 'all-in-all'. Of course, if there were no contact between the knowing subject and the object to be known, then all knowledge would be impossible.

Only God, then, can know reality as a whole and in all its parts, because as the transcendental Creator he is *entirely above* the world and as the immanent principle of conservation of the world he is *entirely in* the world; while we in our knowledge are *partly above* and *partly within* the object which we are striving to know.

The result of our being thus submerged in reality is that reality is for us partly a knowable object and partly a mystery, that it has partly a rational character and partly an irrational one, and that in our efforts to comprehend it, we are always lending to it something of ourselves, thus causing the picture of reality to lose something of its pure objectivity. Thus we can see reality only in profile, as it were, or superficially. We would have to examine all its various profiles or aspects in order to form a complete picture of it, and even then we could not enter into the inner nature or structure of things, nor could they make themselves perceptible to us. Hence our knowledge must always remain imperfect. The various pieces of partial knowledge amassed by us in our study of reality move between two poles or focus on two points which are in a relation of opposition to one another and which seem even to be in contradiction. However, it is our human notions which are in contradiction, and not the corresponding realities. Thus, for instance, we see man as a being who is free and yet not so free, the world as limited and yet unlimited, bodies as composed of simple elements and yet of complex elements. So Kant, in his *Antinomies*, need not have drawn his sweeping conclusion regarding the incompetence of human reason in the transcendental order, had he understood that the conclusions concerning the world arrived at by reason are not intrinsically contradictory but rather in an opposition of polarity to one another.[8]

There are tensions again in the very manner of our knowledge: as for instance between conceptual thought and intuitive knowledge. The whole difficult problem of the relation between science and life rests on this relation of opposition between immobile contemplation and mobile thought.[9]

The opposition between two ways of comprehending things is an opposition of polarity, not an opposition of logical contradiction, that is to say, in which one excludes the other entirely from having any element of truth. Thus, for instance, if a person conceives an object in a certain way, he does not have to deny that there is contained in that object an element which is at opposite poles to his concept. If a person says that the Church is invisible, he does not have to deny that the Church is also visible, since neither of these two concepts seeks to express the whole essence of the Church. The truth is that the essence of the Church lies somewhere between these two concepts used by us to try to comprehend an object which in itself is outside the scope of our human reason. The two concepts might be compared to forceps, with which we try to grasp an object which is too big to be taken between the fingers. It is only by trying to grasp with rational concepts things which are intrinsically and in themselves unknowable that it is at all possible for us to come to know anything about them; if we were unable or unwilling to do this, we would know nothing about them. It is by examining things

[8] Kant himself calls this opposition 'real repugnance' to distinguish it from 'logical repugnance'. 'In speaking of logical repugnance, we mean that relation in virtue of which the predicates of a thing and their consequences destroy each other by reason of the contradiction between them'; real repugnance, on the other hand, is based on 'the relation of two predicates of the same thing which oppose one another', but in such a way that 'the one does not deny what is affirmed by the other.' From *'Versuch, den Begriff der negativen Grössen in die Weltweisheit einzuführen'*, Königsberg 1763, ed. by Ernst Cassirer, Berlin 1912, II p. 210.

[9] In this connection, and for the whole question of opposition, cf. Romano Guardini, *Der Gegensatz, Versuche zu einer Philosophie des Lebendig-Konkreten*, Mainz 1925, published by Grünewald, pp. 202 ff.

from different aspects, which often, though not necessarily, imply a relation of polarity, that the progress of knowledge is at all possible. One may bore a tunnel through an impassable mountain, beginning on both sides simultaneously, and thus conquer it. If we are on the narrow crest of a mountain ridge, we must keep moving if we are to retain our balance and not to fall.

Thus the truth may be said to lie on the razor's edge, that is to say, it is not to be found on any single plane of reality, but at the point of intersection of two planes. There is, for instance, a tension between the two propositions: 'The Church is the realisation of the religious soul' and 'the religious soul is the realisation of the Church.' Each of these propositions is correct provided it does not exclude the correctness of the other. Again, it is equally true to say that 'the whole exists before the parts' and to say that 'the parts exist before the whole.' We are equally justified in speaking of the primacy of the Logos (reason) over the Eros (love) and of the primacy of the Eros over the Logos; for the Church and the believing soul, the whole and the parts, the Eros and the Logos are in a reciprocal relation of tension, which we call a relation of polarity.

The law of tension is not unimportant for our question, in so far as it brings home to us that in the relation of tension existing between religion and life, religion must not deny or despise life and life may not deny or despise religion. In defending the rights of religion, we must not deny life its rights, and vice versa. For if one of the two denies the other its right to existence, then the tension between them falls away, like the bowstring, one end of which is untied; the result is a unilateral exclusiveness, which forms a barrier to any further understanding. To 'grasp' a thing, we need two hands or two fingers, or at least two joints of the one finger, for a thing cannot be grasped from one side alone.

In order that a state of tension may come into being, there must be some element which links the two forces which are in opposition to each other; this holds good in the spiritual and intellectual spheres as in the mechanical sphere. Things which are absolutely foreign to one another can never enter into a relation of tension to one another, because they can never come into contact with one another. Each one rejects the other's very right to existence and by its own existence constitutes an attack upon the other. At all times great men, especially great religious heroes, have been rejected and persecuted because mankind did not understand them and because they were different from the rest of men. For, 'if they had known it, they would never have crucified the Lord of Glory.'[10] And we know too, from our own experience, that when hostility erupts, relations are usually broken off—one party wants 'to have nothing more to do with the other' or 'never wants to speak of him again.'

Between men who are completely foreign to each other in every way, there is no consciousness of a common bond. That which is unfamiliar in nature produces a strange effect on us, because it does not conform to the ordinary pattern of our thinking; thus, for instance, the snake gives us a creepy feeling at first glance, because we see it moving but cannot perceive how it moves. However, he who has become acquainted with the unfamiliar no longer fears it. Following the law that an intrinsic hostility always exists between fundamentally different things or persons, Esau will always persecute his brother Jacob and the just man will suffer persecution. The 'barbarian', that is to say, he who speaks an unfamiliar language, will always provoke a hostile reaction in the primitive type of human being, since the unknown language is regarded as an attack upon his own way of life which is expressed in his native tongue. In order that the 'hostis', the enemy, may come to be regarded as a friend or 'guest',—for both of these words come from the same Indo-Germanic root—he must be seen and recognised as a fellow-man.

He is accepted as a friend and a brother, when he is seen as another of God's family. Again, what is holy and consecrated is at first experienced by men as something strange and different (the *tremendum*) and fills them with awe and terror, but later they come to discern an element of attractiveness in it, (the *fascinosum*) and it awakens in them trust and submission; it is the union of these elements that makes it possible for us to recognise the aspect of holiness and consecration in religious worship, and that sets up a relation of tension between the 'sacred' and the 'profane'.

Tension, then, requires both common and differentiating elements. In the case of man, the common element may be blood relationship, political or social position, commerce, science; the strongest bond of union, however, is religion, that is to say, the relation of man to God. This makes all men akin. All other bonds of union may give way under severe strain

[10] 1 Corinthians 2, 8.

and leave men once again strangers and enemies to one another; but a living religion cannot give way: if it did, it would no longer be living. Nothing could be more tragic or fateful for men, in what pertains to their inner unity and to their union with other men, than to have the common bond of their relationship with God and the world broken off; then a man becomes a stranger to himself and to all his fellow-men.

If the state of tension is to achieve something, it should not be continually broken up. It is neither the state of opposition between the forces nor the state of equilibrium, in themselves, that achieves something, but the fact that the two forces, though opposed, are both striving to arrive at a state of equilibrium. Each one retains its own independence, yet they are freely orientated towards each other. It is not a case of their neutralising each other, as hot and cold water do when they mix to form tepid water, and neither are they related like *autonomy* and *heteronomy*, which come together in the form of *theonomy*, nor are they like the resultant in the parallelogram of forces, which is formed of the sum or the difference of the individual forces. We must not think either in terms of a 'middle way' between them, which treads warily between all obstacles, for this would be no real way of getting anywhere, but an abstract mathematical line. Again, they are not in such a relationship that one force destroys the other by absorbing it into itself, nor are the two forces united in such a way that each one loses its own independence, as when two commercial concerns merge to form a completely new one, nor do they meet each other half-way in the form of a compromise, as when two parties make mutual concessions in order to come to an agreement. They do not unite in the form of a synthesis by forming a third unity, which is higher; nor is it the case that, while remaining intrinsically irreconcilable, they coexist peacefully, thus forming a syncretism, as for instance, when certain elements of doctrine in a religion or church ally themselves together without forming a real organic unity.

Just as a drop of water falling on a surface never travels in a straight line and sound and light always travel through the ether in wave movements, so, too, progress in spiritual activity does not take the form of a straight line, but proceeds by periodic impulses in a continual fluctuation of polar forces. The object moves between these poles to right and left, up and down, back and forward; if ever, however, it withdraws itself from the plane of movement to cling to either of the two poles, then the movement, and with it all hope of progress, comes to a standstill.

This conflict of opposites is a law of life for man and for humanity. Woe betide man and humanity, if they do not heed this law! Woe betide those who languish in a state of complacent stagnation, no matter in what sphere! We have to fight for what we have, in order to possess it ever anew and ever more perfectly.

Conflicts should not be avoided because where there is no conflict there is only stagnation and atrophy. Tension is necessary for the existence, preservation and progress of all living things ; when it is destroyed, death must inevitably follow. In the case of humanity, this tension can be suspended only in an eternal life when no further progress is possible, all possible goals having been attained. But in this life, this continuous interchange between tension and release of energy is necessary for all progress. When one force exerts some energy, it must be answered by an exertion of energy on the part of the opposite force, as for instance in the process of walking. Now it may happen that one of the forces will be more concerned with the preservation or the restoration of equilibrium, while the other will be more intent on pressing forward in some definite direction; but nevertheless, these two tendencies, the analytic and the synthetic, must remain in the proper relation to one another.

The analytic spirit furthers progress by excavating, as it were, from the bosom of the earth the raw materials it contains and heaping up these treasures, while the synthetic spirit then comes along and levels off and shapes these mounds of treasure already at hand. Since it is the initial effort of the analytic spirit that provides the synthetic spirit with the raw material for its work, Count Keyserling is right when he says that it is not universalism but unilateralness which forms the shortest way to totality.[11] But this unilateralness could not take even one step forward if the universalist did not come along to gather and arrange in order the fruits of his labours. The history of political society is a history of conflicts between the different conceptions of the State, the history of civilisation is a history of conflict between nature and culture, the history of the Church is a history of conflict between the religious community and the

[11] Der Leuchter: *Weltanschauung und Lebensgestaltung*, annual publication of '*Schule der Weisheit*', Vol. 4, Darmstadt, Otto Reichl Publications, p. 14.

society by which it was surrounded, the history of economics is a history of the conflict between capital and labour, the history of Christian man is a history of the conflict between religion and life. Christianity was strongest and most vital in the days when there were powerful tensions between it and the other forces in life. When religion arrives at a stage when it is not a living reality but a dead form, and when life is no longer religious but atheistic, then the tension between them is broken and their doom is sealed.

There must, therefore, be tension. It is something which is intrinsically necessary and in accordance with the will of God. There is no such thing as absolute repose. Even when bodies appear to be in a state of equilibrium, their constitutive elements are in a continuous oscillatory movement; our organs of perception are incapable of perceiving this movement, but it is certain that these minute elements, just like the apparently fixed bodies, are always tending towards a state of equilibrium. There is a continual progress from chaos to cosmos, and this holds good in every order of life, even in the spiritual life. Each tension resolves itself in repose only to be followed by a new state of tension, and so the process goes on. The only thing that must be guarded against is that this tension be changed into a state of separation or division, for it is this, not the conflict between the opposing forces, which is to be feared. In this sense it may be said that 'conflict is the father of all things.' Once this conflict or tension is present, we can have confidence that that beneficial law, which obliges us to mobilise all our powers towards the attainment of an ideal unity, will bring about the realisation of fruitfulness and progress; for conflict generates warmth, warmth generates movement, and movement generates life and growth.

Tension in the spiritual life

The law of tension is the key to a most fruitful outlook upon earthly things. The duality of being pervades the entire organisation of the world. In the state of primal chaos there was no unity whatsoever, while at the end of the world, everything will have been restored to a state of unity. In its progress from one of these termini to the other, however, the world is governed by the basic law of duality of matter and form, flesh and spirit, male and female, idea and phenomenon, and countless other realities which are related to one another in

2

a similar way. In each case the tension between the opposing terms is a principle of being and development. It is the way which leads to unity; we can see therefore that Monism contains this one element of truth. This law of polarity is the law which regulates the universe and all of human life, the law by which two things are mutually impelled towards each other and strive to become one, just as in marriage man and wife become 'one flesh'[12] and just as in the kingdom of God 'there is neither Jew nor Greek, slave nor freeman, male nor female, but all are one in Christ.'[13] The final end of all development, complete perfection, consists in the cessation of duality and its giving way to unity.

This idea is beautifully expressed in the so-called second Epistle of St. Clement:[14] 'When the Lord was once asked when his kingdom would come, he replied: "When the two become one, when what is external becomes like that which is internal, when the two sexes become one so that there is neither male nor female." The two, however, are one when we speak the truth one to another and when in two bodies there is but one soul without guile. The external like the internal is to be understood thus: he calls the soul that which is within, the body that which is without. Now just as the body is visible, so, too, the soul must become visible by good works. And the coming together of the sexes so that there will be neither male nor female, means, that when a man meets a woman, he must not look upon her solely as a woman, nor must she look upon him solely as a man. "If you do all these things", said the Lord, "then the kingdom of my Father will come".'

An enumeration of the many tensions which exist in human life leads us to a closer examination of this law of tension and the range of its operations. There is a tension between intuitive and scientific knowledge. Originally, the two existed together side by side in the same subject, in a state of harmony and equilibrium. Primitive wisdom is nothing more than the intuitive knowledge which any man of sound mind acquires. Gradually, however, a spirit of wonder and enquiry sets in, creating a tension, and with it a desire for deeper knowledge in order to resolve that tension. With the resolution of this tension came the joy of knowledge; but it was found that all knowledge contained within its bosom the germs of new problems, just as a light, when it becomes brighter, casts a

---

[12] Genesis 2, 24; [13] Galatians 3, 29.
[14] Second Epistle of St. Clement 12, 2–6.

darker shadow, and thus an infinite process was set in motion. Tension, therefore, is in this case also the principle of progress. The highest wisdom of all is the tranquil possession of a harmonious and unified knowledge which is based on the soundest possible reasoning.

There is likewise a tension in the very methods of scientific knowledge. Dogmatic and unquestioning confidence in the power of our reason to know is followed by an unhealthy and sceptical mistrust of reason, the tension between the two being resolved in a healthy, critical mistrust. Pure dogmatism is stagnation, pure scepticism is decay; in criticism, there must always be a tension between the two, and this tension is the principle of progress in philosophy.

There is a conflict between knowledge and faith. In the ingenuous consciousness of the child, the two are inseparably fused. To the child everything is full of wonder; there is no such thing as a child who does not believe. But then comes the first doubt, some experience conflicts with convictions long held sacred, and with that, the hour of decision has struck. It must now be decided whether blind faith or intellectual pride on the one hand or a reasoned faith on the other will gain the upperhand. Whatever the outcome, it is this tension that advances the progress of religious knowledge. There is a tension between instinct and liberty. The simple morality of the child or of primitive man has not as yet become acquainted with this tension, they live in what we call a state of innocence. Then that 'law of the flesh which opposes the law of the spirit' begins to make itself felt, instinct and liberty come into conflict, and once again, a decision has to be made as to what the outcome will be, a life ruled entirely by carnal instincts, or a life in which these instincts will assume their true proportions; or on the other hand, a life of continual struggle between the two tendencies. It is this struggle which develops personality and which creates a character at once unified and harmonious, enlightened and self-controlled.

There is tension between nature and culture. Originally, the two were inseparable; man lives with nature as a part of it. The hut of primitive man is only a detail of the landscape in which it stands: it breathes in even rhythm with the rest of nature. Primitive culture, then, is identical with the life of nature. Soon, however, the cultural drive begins to be beyond the life of nature, and a tension arises.

Man has now to make a decision: either to tear asunder

the bonds which bind him to nature or to strengthen them evermore; either to return to nature or to adopt a superior culture; either natural culture or cultivated nature, born of the spirit and developed through a perpetual conflict with his own matter and with the elements of nature surrounding him.

There is a tension between the individual and society. A man is born into the community of the family, and it is some time before he becomes aware of the conflict between the two forces. Then, however, he becomes conscious of personal interests and responsibilities. The more he develops, the more alone and independent he becomes and the greater is the tension created between himself and other men. If this tension breaks down, then we have individualism, but if it is resolved in unity, then we have solidarity; in the one case, separation and revolt, in the other, harmony and sense of community. In the person of Jesus Christ we have the most striking individualism, even to the point that he claimed the name of Son of God for himself alone and put himself on a par with God; simultaneously we have the finest expression of solidarity in that he gave his life for others. Individualism is not altered by the fact of individuals coming together for the attainment of their individual ends; even socialism is only a collective individualism because it does not give rise to any inner community spirit. It is equally true, however, that solidarity is not altered by the fact that a man retains his own individual character or that he cultivates his own national, intellectual or social life. The citizen, who is bound in solidarity with his fellowmen, does not thereby feel himself obliged to be a citizen of the world: in other words one who would reduce all the heights and depths of human society to the same level.

But society itself is also faced with a similar problem, namely, whether it is to be just a mass or a society. When a man is completely absorbed by the community he becomes a mere unit of the mass. On the other hand when he rejects society he causes a revolution. The outcome of the tension between the individual person and the community must be a conscious and ever-vigilant integration and submission of personal interests to the community, in such a way that the community does not suppress the personality of the individual and the individual does not conspire against society. Then the tension becomes a principle of prosperity and of progress.

There is a conflict in the Church between community and society. Originally this was scarcely adverted to at all: there

was a state of equilibrium between the two, and their content
and form were accommodated to each other. As the organism
grew, however, conflicts arose, making it necessary for the
moral precepts, dogmas and laws of the Church to be
formulated. Now this tension may lead to a trend in the
direction of Gnosis (unbridled development), or to a dry and
lifeless orthodoxy, which is mere form without content. It
may also lead however to an uninterrupted conscious submission of the spiritual man to the law and to the application
of that law to souls. The latter way is the means by which
the best energies of the soul can be exercised.

The law of tension operates in the same way in respect of
the mutual relations between tradition and progress, dogma
and research, State and Church, authority and freedom,
autonomy and heteronomy, nature and art, experience and
intuition, possession and conquest.

The ideal goal is always that of equilibrium between
opposites. But in order to arrive at that goal, there must be
a continual interplay between the opposing forces. The goal
of all tensions is repose, but this repose lies in infinity. It is not
the cessation of all conflicts nor is it an enduring truce in the
struggle, but rather a reposeful activity and an active repose.
At the end of his development, man has come back again to
his original starting-point, the only difference being that the
unity, which at the beginning he accepted unconsciously, he
now comprehends consciously. This is the truth which is contained in the sublime words of the Lord: 'Unless you become as
little children, you cannot enter into the kingdom of heaven.'

Starting from the unselfconscious innocence of childhood,
we return by way of the battle between conflicting forces to
the unity and harmony of a conscious childhood. In this whole
process of tensions being set up, resolved and succeeded by
further tensions, there are no predetermined moments of
climax in time; and this is how spiritual growth is different
from organic growth. Organic growth is directed towards a goal
which is predetermined and already known, after which comes
decay. In the spiritual life, however, there is no decay and no
final stage, save that God in his grace has set a goal to it,
which is its complete fulfilment in the vision and possession of
infinity, that is, of himself. But the more we strive towards
this goal, the more it recedes into infinity. Truly great spirits
have recognised this state of things and have learned humility
from it; wise men and saints have always had a deep conviction

that the ideal of knowledge, as of sanctity, is lost in infinity, just as the horizon always recedes from whosoever imagines he can reach it.

This law of repose holds not only for individual men but also for human communities and for mankind in general. In this connection, the basic law of bio-genetics is valid to a certain extent, namely, that ontogenesis is a brief and rapid recapitulation of phylogenesis: in other words, that the development of the individual human being reproduces that of humanity; and the reverse is also true: that phylogenesis is a slow and long drawn out repetition of the process of ontogenesis, or, the development of humanity is a repetition of the development of the individual human being. First harmony, then conflict, resulting either in disharmony or else in conscious harmony; first unity, then divergence, being resolved in division or conscious unity. Just as in the most rudimentary organisms, for instance the lower algae, it is impossible to distinguish between the male and female cells, a distinction which becomes visible only in higher organic forms, so, too, in the spiritual life of man and of humanity, religion and life are scarcely distinguishable initially since the religious element and the life of nature form a unity which it is very difficult for the adult or the enlightened mind to analyse. Only gradually does a visible duality emerge. But the final end of this duality, as of all development, is the restoration of harmony. The ancients, in a way peculiar to themselves, conceived the union of the physical and the spiritual as a reflection of the harmony of the spheres, making the harmony of the celestial bodies serve as an image of the unity and repose of human knowledge.

The history of philosophy furnishes another instance of this process of development. The first scientific attempts bore a theological character; the first cosmogonies, for instance, were fables and myths of the pagan gods. Then the various branches of science came by degrees to set themselves up more or less consciously against theology and popular religion, but this subsequently gave way to a tendency to bring themselves into harmony with theology by means of a more profound insight into the relations between them, and without prejudice to their own independence. In the history of culture likewise, we can perceive a tension between the culture of noble sensibility, as amongst the Greeks, and a culture of pure spirituality, as in the early years of Christianity. The link, which makes a tension between them possible, is that the two, sensibility and spirituality, were each cultivated without the total exclusion of the other one. Just as in the domain of philosophy, dogmatism is followed by scepticism and the two are resolved in a healthy criticism, so also it often happens to mature spirits that, after having passed through the stages of ingenuous belief and conscious disbelief, they draw continuously closer to the old forms of thought, which are in harmony with faith.[15] In any sound physical or moral organism, tension and repose must follow each other in such a way that more and more potential energy is being transformed into kinetic energy, thereby constantly heightening the value of the organism which has within itself these forces in a state of tension.

Tension between religion and life

The law of tension has a special and very beneficial application in the matter of the relation which exists between religion and life. Religion and life are both elemental forces. The very fact that they both lay claim to the entire man and to all men and human institutions, immediately sets up a state of tension between them. This tension is not between God and the world, or between nature and grace: in the first place, the world is not autonomous and cannot be regarded as something entirely outside of God, nor is there any such thing as a nature which is an independent entity opposed to grace; in the second place, there is no parity between these related terms in such a way that a state of tension could be communicated from one to the other. The tension consists in the fact that one and the same man finds himself wooed by two opposing forces, each of which wants to take entire possession of him: on the one hand the world and its values, into which he was born and of which he forms a part by his very nature, and on the other hand, the supernatural, into which he has been incorporated by God.

In other terms the tension is between the world of God and the God of the world, between nature elevated to the state of grace and grace which has descended into the state of nature. In this tension between religion and life, we do not have religion alone without life nor life alone without religion, but living religion and religious life. The two forces which are in tension,

[15] Cf. Max Ettlinger, *Philosophische Fragen der Gegenwart*, Kempten and Munich 1911, Kösel Publishing Co., pp. 277–303.

religion and life, have at the same time something in common
and something which puts them at variance with one another.
If they were totally different, then they would mutually
exclude each other and any relationship between them would be
impossible if they were identical, they could enter into no real
relation, only a logical relation. The element which they have
in common is that they both belong to human nature: true
religion is also life and true life is also religion. They are different
and yet there is a strong affinity between them. If they were
in absolute opposition to each other, then either human nature
would be totally destroyed by being swallowed up in religion,
as in the case of Hindu mysticism, or else life would suppress
religion altogether, as in the case of pure humanism; in any
case, there could be no tension set up between them, since the
one would be a negation of the other.

Now the further the positive pole is from the negative, the
greater will be the tension between them, and the greater the
tension, the greater will be the energy released by the discharge
of that tension and the work which can utilise that energy.
The more closely, then, a man is in contact with the earth,
the more closely must he cling to the things of Heaven; the
more he devotes himself to the cultural enterprises of this
world, the more must he be rooted in religion. The contrary
holds true also; the more a man lives among divine and eternal
values, the more must he devote himself to the values of this
world, which are for him an image of the heavenly values, and
the more must he endeavour to sanctify them. If he is not
firmly rooted in God, then he must inevitably be swallowed up
in worldliness. If he forgets that his feet are on this earth, then
he becomes the victim of an exaggerated and sterile mysticism.
If culture wished to replace Christianity or to set it aside
entirely, then it would lose all its power; on the other hand, if
a christian thought to emancipate himself entirely from the
eternal laws of nature, his christianity would become a mere
salt without savour.

When religion is understood in its purest sense as the relation
of man to a transcendent God and the submission of the entire
man to him, and when life is understood in all its vitality as
the highest possible cultivation of the values of this world,
and when both of them do, in fact, govern man and all human
relations, then the tension reaches its climax with a consequent
release of energy, the maximum amount of work and progress
being achieved. The alternation of tension and repose is most

fruitful when it is in the form of a steady oscillatory movement, that is, a movement which approaches now the one, now the other pole, but which remains all the while within the two poles of God and the world. The alternation between tension and repose, between charge and discharge, introduces an element of disquiet and of sorrow into life. The conversion of potential into kinetic energy is a continual process of dying and being reborn. To see on the screen, for instance, the growth, bloom and decay of a plant compressed into a few seconds makes one realise that the rhythm of life is accompanied by a continual cry of pain, the world moans from the birth-pangs of every new stage of development. And if this is true of the life of Nature's organisms, it is also true in this matter of the relationship between religion and life.

In the true Christian the tension between religion and life reaches its maximum, because being fully aware of his vocation to arrive at union with God, he feels in the keenest possible way a longing for the realisation of this union, while at the same time, as a man, this same vocation strengthens his awareness of the strong ties which bind him to the earth. And since both forces tend of their very nature to take complete control of man, there must inevitably be inner struggles and crises all along the way, for the one man is wooed by two opposing forces and feels himself torn between them.

The tension between them flows, therefore, from the very nature of life and religion. Religion, as the relation of man to God, strains towards God as its ultimate end and desires nothing more than to conquer or remove all obstacles, in order to give itself to him in a state of perfect repose, for repose is the goal of all motion. Life, however, with all its allure, its spiritual and sensible values, draws the 'man of earth' under its spell and strives to take complete possession of him. The more perfect his love for God and the stronger the urge in him toward the life of earth, the greater will be the tension between the two. Religion strains towards the fulfilment of his longing for God, while life strains towards the development of his own nature.

Pure nature leads us to the true God, and pure religion leads us to a true nature. To the simple and unspoiled man everything speaks of God, and only the truly religious man understands the language of nature. The following can be stated as a proposition: the more a person is estranged from nature, the more he is estranged from God; and likewise, the nearer we are to God, the more intimately we feel the relationship between ourselves and all the things of nature. Everything which estranges a man from nature estranges him also from God, and everything which brings a man nearer to God brings him nearer also to nature. The technological and industrial stamp of modern life has served to cut off industrial man and the city-dweller from the normal activities of nature. He scarcely ever sees the sun rise, he may never see a waving field of corn, he seldom sees the starry heavens. In the light of electric street lamps he never experiences the ambrosian beauty of the night and in the roar of the traffic he can never savour the tranquillity of solitude. The bread, that he eats, did not grow upon his fields; everything around him is the product of human industry or ingenuity and does not carry the immediate imprint of God's creative hand. God is no longer visible to him behind the things of the world.

The man who lives in intimate union with nature is nearer to God. Everything speaks to him of God, he knows that he is dependent on the divine favour for everything. There is no such thing as a people living close to nature and yet unbelieving. Lack of belief is found only amongst men who have been estranged from nature by a false civilisation. Conversely, religion also leads to nature, in the sense that it is only from the divine viewpoint that one can see the works of God properly. When one knows a master-tradesman or an artist, one can discern characteristic features in his work and so understand the work better than another person who sees it not as the work of a particular individual, but as a mere object. In the same way, the reality of the world is better understood as God's creation than merely as something which exists. The normal human being is continually under the successive influences of human and divine life.

The problem of religion and life is not simply a problem of our time. It concerns all men in every age and in every instant of their lives. Man and mankind live by the struggle of opposites, a struggle which has for its final end either the eternal repose which comes from complete possession, or else ruin and decay. But ruin cannot be the final destiny of the world, and there can be no eternal peace or repose in this world, only in a world beyond this one. It is not granted to this world and to the man who lives in this world to enjoy perfect repose, neither have we a duty to attain complete happiness in this world. The only thing that is granted to us is a relative repose in the certainty that we are striving to create equilibrium out of tension. The harmony of human life is not a natural harmony, but a tragic harmony in the sense that it is a harmony produced by tensions. The struggle is a source of joy and strength by its very nature, as being a free play of forces and being accompanied by the certainty of victory and reward. But a state of spiritual distress can arise, when the forces of tension which are related to each other threaten to separate entirely, and that is what is happening at the present time. And this situation means that we are drifting into spiritual perils which were never experienced to the same extent in earlier times.

2
The separation
between religion and life

The final end of all development is unity and repose, and yet the way to this end lies through a series of tensions. Tension, therefore, is a law of life, and one which operates for good. Now there is, in actual fact, a separation between religion and life at this very time. It is true, of course, that there has always been a divergence between the ideal and the reality of life, between what ought to be and what actually is, and it seems to be the fate of truth, as of Christianity itself, that only a very few ever come to fully understand it and to apply it to the realities of life. One might almost be tempted to speak of the failure of Christianity and to say that God's redemptive work was done in vain. Everything which is great becomes small in the hands of men, and Leibnitz[1], advances the view that the greater number of men has always indentified religion with ritual formalities, and that true piety, that is to say, the piety founded on knowledge and virtue, has never been part of its heritage.

The same thought is voiced by Cardinal Newman,[2] who says that Christianity has had little success in the hearts of the masses and that their attitude to spiritual matters has changed little since pagan times; the life of the large city is much the

[1] *Die Theodizee*, Preface I, Robert Habs. Edition in Reclam series, P. 46.

[2] J. H. Cardinal Newman, *A Newman Synthesis*, extracts from his works, compiled by Erich Przywara, S.J. with an introduction by Przywara and translation by Otto Karrer, S.J., Vol. 6, Freiburg 1922.

same to-day as in any other age, and all classes of society, both high and low, show so little difference from what they would have been even without a knowledge of the Gospel, that one can scarcely speak at all of any success of Christianity; the conduct of men in trade and science, in civil and political life, still follows the old pagan ways. However, the Cardinal adds, there have been at all times chosen souls who served the truth, saints who formed the nucleus of the Church, a body of sanctified souls, ever growing in number and forming the hope of the future. At no time or place in the history of mankind do we find the synthesis of religion and life realised. In this respect Jesus stands upon a peak alone. However, never has the separation between religion and life been so deep as to-day. In fact we can speak of a Christian culture only with certain reservations.

Of course, it would be going too far in the other direction to say that Christianity has no influence on life. It is not that there is no longer any Christianity, but rather that it falls short of the influence on the life of the world which is its right and which it is God's will that it should exercise. It is only by a comparison with a society, completely untouched by any breath of religion, that one could realise what religion means to humanity. But no such society exists, not even outside Christianity, and certainly not in Europe. A person who completely ignores religion would, in our culture, be like a vegetarian in the midst of meat-eaters or a temperance advocate in the midst of drinkers. [3] Everything around him would remind him of religion: the churches in city and town and the little chapels on the lonely hillside; the wayside crosses and the pictures on livingroom walls; the very names we bear, the feasts we celebrate, many proverbs and even the very oaths of popular speech.

In the last analysis, there is no one whose whole attitude to life does not centre around religion, no matter whether he professes it or scoffs at it. It is only the last world war and the moral catastrophe which it brought in its train upon the culture of Europe and of the whole world, that has brought it home to us how little we can really call ourselves Christians. But even this realisation itself is a great grace.

[3] Cf. Friedrich Naumann, *Briefe über Religion*, Berlin 1916, G. Reimer, p. 10.

UNITY AND TENSION IN THE CHRISTIAN PAST

The early Christian years

To trace this separation between religion and life, we need to take a glance at the very beginnings of Christianity. Even then there was a certain opposition between it and the cultural life of the time. With the coming of Jesus, a new era had burst upon the world, but his work remained incomplete—the millenium, the new man, the new humanity, the kingdom of God, had not yet appeared. Failing to grasp Christ's intention of leaving to men themselves the task of bringing his work to completion, the early Christians continued to fix their gaze with longing on Heaven, whence the Saviour would finally return to establish and assume his regal dominion. The disciples, who were united in their faith in the risen Christ and who had experienced the wonders of Pentecost, were 'not so much a body, existing in a definite time and space, as a community of souls clinging to the memory of the glorified Christ and looking forward with hope and expectation to the enjoyment of their rights as citizens of Heaven.'[4] This nostalgic longing for the joys of Heaven, which pulsates through all the writing of the first two centuries, pushed the earth and the things of this earth into the background. The awareness of the new revelation and the new spiritual life forced all else into the background. Christianity was as if dazzled by the new light. It needed time to awaken out of this ecstasy and find its way back to the realities of earth. Only gradually did the realisation grow that the winning of the world for God was not a task for God alone but also one for nascent Christianity.

Christianity, at that stage, was not immediately concerned with cultural work. The world, for it, is encompassed by iniquity. It is seen as the concupiscence of the eyes, the lusts of the flesh and the pride of life; and the disciple's first care must be to keep himself from being contaminated by it. An ancient Christian prayer 'Maranatha' (Come, O Lord) gives expression to this suppressed longing for the Second Coming of the Lord;

[4] Adolf von Harnack, *Die Entstehung der christlichen Theologie und des kirchlichen Dogmas*, Gotha 1927, Leopold Klotz, p. 6.

and St. Paul admonishes: 'And be not conformed to this world'[5]
and again: '.. they also who have wives, be as if they had none ;
and they that weep, as though they wept not; and they that
rejoice, as though they rejoiced not; and they that buy, as
though they possessed not; and they that use this world, as if
they used it not: for the fashion of this world passeth away.'[6]
In the Didaché, or the 'Teaching of the Twelve Apostles', a work
from the end of the first century which may be described as the
first Catechism, we find the prayer: 'May grace come and
may this world pass away.'[7] Tertullian also writes in his
'Apologeticus'[8] : 'The only thing about this world which
concerns us is to leave it as quickly as possible.'

This is not the same as the contempt for the world which
we find in the wisdom of the Indian sages, for whom the world
was a thing evil in itself; because Christianity never forgot that
the world was a creation of God. But in the expectation of
the eagerly longed for treasures of Heaven the world simply
receded. Even the doctrine of Jesus was not concerned with
culture; his mission was higher than any mere cultural or
social or even moral mission. He also speaks of the world in
terms of contempt, even hate, nevertheless it always remain
for him the world of his Father, made in his likeness. When
therefore, we speak of the hostility of early Christianity to
the world, we mean either the conflict between the new life
and the wicked world, or else the hostility which may be said
to exist between what is good and what is better; there is
never any question of a pessimistic philosophy of life. The
expectation of the Second Coming was born of the eagerness
with which the first Christians, deeply moved by the new
revelation, longed for the kingdom of God, but it was not
an essential article of doctrine—had it been so, the young
Christian Church could not have so easily overcome its dis-
appointment at seeing the Second Coming so long delayed.

This attitude to the world was not without its fortunate
consequences for the young Church, and indeed may well have
been in the designs of Providence. It gave the religious mission
of Christianity time to gain a foothold and to establish itself
without being compromised or turned aside from its path by
the love of this world. Christianity was not a mere cultural
movement but a real religious revival. It is worthy of note, too,
that the Platonic philosophy, which prevailed in those early
days, with its teaching of ideas as the only reality, of which

[5] Romans 12, 2; [6] 1 Corinthians 7, 29–31; [7] 10, 6; [8] ch. 41.

the world is only an imperfect reflection, was also conducive
to this attitude of turning away from the world. Its theory
that the union of soul and body, by which man was formed,
was a mere external one and imposed on him by way of
punishment, was favourable to this religious attitude which
fixed its gaze solely upon a higher world. This view of the
world and of the soul lives on in the theology of the Alexandrine
and later in that of the Jansenists.

Gradually, then, Christianity realised the magnitude and
importance of the task which awaited it in the world, and with
all the optimism of youth and the abundant spiritual vigour
which it had stored up in the seclusion of the early years, it
turned towards the world with courage and self-confidence and
created a Christian culture. In contrast to the East, which had
given itself over almost completely to the world-hating and
barren teaching of Gnosticism, the Church of Rome, inheriting
the sober and realistic genius of the Roman people, was able
to adapt its teaching to this world without sacrificing anything
of its eschatological significance. As early as the 2nd century,
we can see emerging the idea of reconciling religious duties
with the obligations imposed by living in this world. Clement of
Alexandria (c.150–216) is the first theologian to see this as
one of the pressing problems of the age: he formulates it
expressly and tries to solve it. For him the solution lies in
Christ, in the eternal divine reason, as the model for the human
race, that is to say, in the *Christos logos paidagogos*. Against
the enemies of Christianity, who sneered at it as a religion
fit for slaves and for the uncultured masses, it was necessary to
show that Christianity contained the germs of true civilisation
for the world and of a more elevated and profound cultural
life. It is clear, then, that the young Church of that time had
faced up to the problem of religion and life in the world, even
if it had not yet worked out any final and complete solution.'

The middle ages

With the entry of the Germanic peoples into the historic
picture, the problem of religion and life raised its head again
and the Church in the Middle Ages exerted itself manfully to
create a cultural unity. The religion of classical Greece, on the
one hand, was so much in touch with the world that even its
temples had no sanctuary, the statues of the gods being plainly
visible and accessible to all. On the other hand, the Church

of the Catacombs was a church of pure interior life, which had withdrawn into secluded communion with Christ, whose presence was felt even though incorporeally, and whose power pervaded the whole community. Now in the Middle Ages we see this interior life bursting forth from the seclusion of the Catacombs to straightaway set about impressing its own character on all creation. It aimed at nothing less than an entire reshaping of everything around it. The Middle Ages produced in the West a Christian culture, characterised to a large extent by the unity of which we have been speaking; without the Church this culture would not have been possible. [9] To us, who have once again lost this unity, the Middle Ages shine forth as the infancy of Christian culture in Europe, and it was the naive and unspoiled Germanic peoples, themselves in their infancy, who laid the foundations of this culture.

Like the child for whom everything is an object of wonder, the medieval man saw the power and the guiding hand of God in everything, and did not trouble himself about the natural laws through which God allows his power to operate. However this linking of religion and life, naive as it may seem, was really more true and enlightened than the theories about the world and life evolved by later ages which failed to look beyond Nature for the divinity and allowed God to be supplanted by natural laws. That the Middle Ages recognised this fundamental unity of religion and life is all the more remarkable when we consider the many factors which were opposed to any such recognition: the residue of their newly cast off paganism, the primitive instincts which still seethed in these peoples but lately drawn into the ambit of Christian culture, and which still make themselves felt even in matters of religion; the fact that many peoples, who had been compelled to accept the Faith by political pressure or at the point of the sword instead of being won for Christianity by a gradual evangelisation, were only half aware of the truths of Christianity and had only a very weak grasp of its spirituality; the repeated lapses of the clergy and the Orders into unchristian worldliness and the many sad chapters in the history of the Popes, the relentless struggles between Papacy and Empire and the terrible scandal which they afforded to Christianity; the fundamental differences

---

[9] Cf. Gustav Schnürer, *Kirche und Kultur im Mittelalter*, Vols. I & II, esp. I 139–402 and II 373–407, Paderborn 1924 & 1926, Ferd. Schöningh.——Georg Grupp, *Kulturgeschichte des Mittelalters*, II 1923 and III 1924, Paderborn, Ferd. Schöningh.

between the Germanic and the Roman soul and the tendency of the German to over-subtle religious speculations and to individualism in every sphere.

Never at any time has thought and life and every facet of human and social relationships been so permeated and dominated by christianity as in the Middle Ages. The Middle Ages had a unified total conception of the world and of the duties of men in relation to that world, however much the ideal may sometimes have exceeded the reality.

It must be conceded that this unified concept of life was easier for the medieval man than for the man of today. This unity of religion and life was not the mature unity of a highly developed culture and perfected religious system. In this infancy of the Germanic peoples, neither side had made such great progress that there could be any marked divergence between them. And even in the Middle Ages, we speak of a unified culture only with reservations, for the reason that the term has not a single definite meaning but rather embraces a very complex mass of scientific, moral, religious and economic factors. Even in the Middle Ages gross superstition, immorality and ignorance were to be found alongside the most enlightened knowledge of God and the most noble mysticism, the most pure love of fellowmen and a truly Christian civic spirit. That which chiefly distinguished the Christian Middle Ages from the culture of our time, however, was the fact that it never invoked the principles of Christianity to justify perversions of education, morality, science or physical culture, as our times are in the habit of doing. Injustice was injustice, sin was sin and no attempt was made to throw a religious or ethical cloak over it. The Middle Ages had the advantage of having received both Christianity and culture from the same source, that of the Church, and there had not been the time for the two to go their separate ways, as was to happen later.

This unity in the life of the Middle Ages was more a natural, unselfconscious attitude than a clear realisation of a task to be fulfilled. We see a fundamental unity of theology and philosophy as well as of theological learning and popular belief; there was harmony between Canon Law and Civil Law, between excommunication by the Church and outlawry by the State, between Church feasts and secular festivals, between the cult of the Madonna and the convention of courtly love, between liturgy and the theatre, between the pious brother-hoods or confraternities and the trade guilds, between charity and philanthropy. We may smile to-day at the fact that those who built bridges, had roads made, conferred some endowment on the Church or did some such work for the public good, were as likely to be rewarded by indulgences as by tax exemptions; but it was just another instance of this fusion of grace and nature. The mind of the medieval man saw everything as a service done for the advancement of the kingdom of God. The emperor received his anointing from the hands of the Pope, his ceremonial regalia were inspired by liturgical vestments. The 'Holy Roman Empire of the German nation' was also an expression of this harmony between worldly dominion and the kingdom of God.

This unity between the broad domains of religion and life, Christianity and culture, was the basis of the harmony and peace which prevailed within these several spheres, and in particular amongst the people. Because, even though there were at that time also varying levels of education, there was no such thing as the gulf which yawns to-day between the life of the masses and the bourgeois culture. To-day culture is something which is set up on a pedestal by those who regard themselves as the cultured classes, while it is regarded with envy or contempt by the masses who do not understand it. But just as the great 'Summas' of the Middle Ages combined faith and science, dogma and morality, asceticism and mysticism, so too did the medieval man know how to reconcile the things of earth and those of heaven in his daily life. In the domain of science as in that of philosophy, it was St. Thomas who made the hitherto most successful attempt to show the parallel nature of the forces in faith and science, being and effect, God and the world, nature and grace.

By comparison with antiquity, the Middle Ages is the age of maturity, in which the two poles with which we are concerned have been brought into a state of equilibrium for the time being. But this equilibrium carried within itself the seeds of future tensions. A day had to come when what until then was accepted as natural and taken for granted became the source of new problems and when the opposing poles which had been brought into a state of equilibrium began to go divergent ways and to produce new tensions. Christianity had considerably ennobled medieval man and had done a lot to encourage fruitful and happy human relationships. Under its guiding and protecting hand, mankind had, as it were, come of age. But now a development entered in, which was to be fraught with disturbing consequences! The various domains of the human spirit wished to attain independent existence, and began to strive for freedom and autonomy.

Just as under the political domination of England, the colonial territories, having gradually attained to a certain cultural level, then became conscious of their own strength and began to wish to break with the mother country, so too the various domains of human culture, which had flourished under the wise guidance of the Church, wished to make themselves independent. But they broke away from the maternal hand of the Church before they had attained the inner maturity which is necessary for such independence; they left their maternal home without the blessing of their mother. In many ways their fate seems not unlike that of the prodigal son.

Since the renaissance

In itself, the fact of these several domains of life becoming independent would not be any harm, as it would be only a differentiation of the kind which must necessarily accompany the growth of every living organism. The trouble is that this process got under way prematurely, as we have seen, and that it set up an opposition between life and Christianity. I am not primarily thinking here of the divisions within European Christianity, for instance the Reformation, though, of course, it also has its origin in the same thing, but of the spiritual apostasy from Christianity of the culture of Europe, which goes much deeper than a mere external schism. I am thinking of the great upheaval of values, which, beginning with the Renaissance, gradually came to pervade all departments of the cultural life of Europe and led to their estrangement from religion and from Christianity.[10]

This is a process which begins from above and operates downward. But the upheaval of values, of which we have been speaking, could not have been brought about from above, if there had not been already some undermining influences at work to weaken these values in the main body of European Christianity. The upper classes in any society, and its leaders, correspond to the level of that society in which they set the tone, and vice versa, every society has the government which

[10] Compare Georg Grupp, *Die Verweltlichung des Lebens in der Neuzeit*, Paderborn, Ferd. Schöningh, p. 7 ff.

it deserves. Hence if evil and corruption exist in any society, it is not explained away by saying that it was imposed on the people by their leaders, as all these leaders can do is to map out the plan of campaign and devise practical justifications for the evil which was already existing amongst the members of their society. It is then ideas which come down from above, and which foster the latent evils which are festering in the body of the society; and these ideas seem to have a law of gravity of their own, which brings them down from the apex of the pyramid, which is so often used to represent society, to the base of the pyramid, that is to say, to the lowest stratum of that society. It may take a long time for these ideas to reach the lower strata of the society and begin to work their mischief there; they may be compared to a mountain stream, which, rushing down from the heights, only begins to reveal its full powers in the plains, where it brings either blessing and fruitfulness or floods and destruction.

Now it would be wrong, however, to say that, from the very beginning and in all its great figures, the Renaissance applied itself consciously to effecting this separation; on the contrary, it may be said that the most genuine champions of revived classical forms were well-intentioned men, whose sole desire was to enrich religion, or who at any rate were not hostile to it In fact, many were kept from pagan degeneracy, especially in the domain of morals, by that very sense of law and form, which was native to the genius of Rome. There were ardent champions and defenders of Christianity even among the humanists, St. Thomas More for instance.[11]

The same may be said of the Baroque Age, which was a later off-shoot of the Renaissance. No one who surveys with understanding the age of Catholic Baroque, with its mighty architecture and painting and its magnificent Jesuit institutes of learning, can fail to be amazed at the strong and vibrant faith in life and culture, which still prevailed at that time. 'A note of joyous zest for life pervades the Christian humanism of Catholic Baroque, something of the optimism of Leibnitz, for whom the harmony of the universe was only the expression of a necessary pre-established harmony, serene, joyous and "clothed with grace". We find monks composing litanies in praise of human nature, extolling the beauties of Nature and of Art, of flowers and music, of enchanting perfumes and of feminine graces, and glorifying Christianity as the completion

[11] Grupp, loc. cit., 16 ff.

of the natural man and his natural perfections.'[12] Nevertheless, by and large, the European man of the Renaissance proved incapable of combining this positive optimistic attitude to life with a fervent interior life. And it is not only in Reformation lands that this phenomenon manifests itself; it finds expression in a particularly passionate way in 'The Tragic Sense of Life'[13] by the Spanish poet and philosopher, Miguel de Unamuno, for whom the only solution is a firm reaffirmation of the demands of religious feeling in face of inexorable reason. His expression is much the same as that of Jacobi: 'In the mind a gentile, in the heart a Christian.'

This movement of separation, of which we speak, may be said to have come from below and worked its way upward in another sense, inasmuch as its point of departure was the most vital and basic factor in the life of society, namely, the relations of States to one another and of the citizens to the State. The principles, enunciated by Machiavelli in his book 'The Prince' (Libro del Principe), orientate everything in life towards the State, which is seen as the ultimate source of all Right and Law, and teach a system of political thought, in which there is no place for conscience. His work is the school from which all the power politics of later ages were evolved.

Then it is the turn of philosophy to break loose; hitherto it had been the handmaid of Theology in accordance with the principles of Scholasticism, but now it divorces itself completely from Theology. With the discovery of Nature and of Man, the sciences threw off their allegiance to Theology, hitherto acknowledged as their queen, and became independent. With the passage of time, the position of the theological faculties in the Universities became more and more constrained; the sacred sciences withdrew into the monasteries and wherever they did remain in the increasingly secularized universities, they had to be content with mere toleration. The flourishing University system of the Middle Ages and of the early Renaissance, which had grown to full stature under the wise and far-sighted tutelage of the Church and of the religious Orders and with the material assistance of a generous Catholic people, now withered away and could not compete with the proud new foundations of the secular spirit.

[12] Hans Andrè, *Die Kirche als Keimzelle der Weltvergöttlichung*, a systematic essay proceeding from biological considerations, Leipzig 1920, Vier-Quellen Publishing Co., p. 94.
[13] Munich 1926, Meyer and Jessen.

To realise the extent of the de-christianisation of these institutes of learning at that time, we need only take a look at some of our Catholic Universities of the present day, with their self-effacing buildings and inadequate pedagogical equipment, their small number of students and their ghetto-like retirement from the public gaze, as compared with the flourishing state of their secular counterparts. The hostile response, which the anti-Modernist manifestoes of Pius X met with in the Universities in the years 1907 and 1910, showed how the passage of centuries had only widened the gulf between Theology, especially Catholic Theology, and the profane sciences. It is true that, since then, it has come to be acknowledged in many quarters that Theology belongs to the corpus of the sciences, but it has never completely won back its former position. Every department of learning has been dogged by the continual conflict between science and Faith. The problem of reconciling the Bible with the findings of the natural sciences was for long a source of the most violent disputes and the doctrine of evolution was quite unjustifiably made use of to attack faith and the Church's teaching. The whole atmosphere of the times has been one of subjectivism, voluntarism, positivism and indifferentism, which are the fruits of the exaltation of reason and the rejection of faith in the last century. The very name 'freethinker' is a reflection of the separation between religion and the secular sciences.

Even morality has broken away from religion. We have seen the rise of societies for ethical culture, principally in North America but also in France, England and Germany. Sexual life, in particular, seems to have shaken off every religious norm; and physical love has become poisoned since it attained this autonomy: instead of creating new life, the end of its very nature, it has become a destroyer of life.

In the economic life of society, the principles of Christianity have also been largely lost sight of. Might and not Right is the chief weapon in the struggle between Capital and Labour. There is no department of modern life from which religion has been so ruthlessly and successfully banished as this one. Literature and Art are also disowning any moral and religious norms, and Music and Drama, which owe so much to the Church, are striking out for their own independence and regarding religion as something which does not concern them or against which they must struggle. The mission of the theatre to foster human dignity is no longer acknowledged. At the present day we see the schools and popular education being weaned away from the principles of the Church and also to a great extent from Christianity and religion. Unceasing efforts are being made, especially by various liberal societies, to introduce into the schools a form of undenominational moral instruction in place of the present system of religious instruction, based on the denomination of each child. The long drawn-out conflicts over this question have caused so much bitterness that the Church can never hope for complete success in achieving its aims in the matter: the most it can hope for is that a state of more or less favourable compromise can be arrived at.

This bitter dissension over the question of the schools, with Church, State, teachers and parents all quarelling violently over their rights in the matter, was unknown in the Middle Ages, when all parties were united by religion and did not feel themselves to be enemies and adversaries. Not only was there an absence of strife, but the parties actually vied with one another in furthering this sacred cause which was common to all. It is true that during the period of Enlightenment and of Romanticism there was a revival of the medieval spirit and religion won back some of the influence it had lost. It is sufficient to mention the names of Bishop Sailer and of Joseph von Gorres, but the two movements were fundamentally too little religious to be able to consolidate this influence, which faded away after only a few decades. Again, the reaction to the Kulturkampf movement in Germany did produce an intense religious reawakening but it made no decisive contribution towards bringing about a more intimate relationship between religion and life. It was too much a defensive movement, too preoccupied with manoeuvres of state and ecclesiastical politics to work out for itself a firm and convincing stand on spiritual questions.

The Renaissance saw the start of a vast process of secularisation, which affected all the values of human life, a process which was further developed by the Reformation. With the Reformation the Catholic Church became the Church of Rome and Catholicism was reduced to the status of just one among many other religious sects. Max Fischer says,[14] 'The Faith, the Church's greatest treasure, and the culture of Europe, which were still a unity in the minds of Dante's contemporaries, have drifted away from one another in a way which is painful

[14] *Das Weltbild Dantes*, Mainz 1923, Matthias Grünewald Publishing Co.

to witness; and indeed it is not at all rare to find them opposing one another in insoluble conflict.' Life sets no great store by religious values any longer; and we have the spectacle of Christian and non-Christian cultures, not to speak of individuals and families, existing side by side without really understanding each other's viewpoints or ideologies. There are certain regions here and there where the life of the people is intimately bound up with their religion, for instance the rural districts of Southern Germany and Switzerland and the mountain regions of the Tyrol; we see evidence of this in the happy relationships between the family and the parish, in the painting and decoration of the houses, in the liturgy of the Church and in the customs of everyday life, in the wayside shrines and chapels, in the images of the saints in field and forest. But this is such a rarity for the man who is forced to live in the midst of the present-day cultural set-up that he is inclined to look on it, wherever he does meet it, as something quaint and old-fashioned and 'romantic'.

It is however in these regions, towns, and families, which have remained faithful to their age-old traditions, that there has been most resistance to the de-christianisation of daily life and the separation of life from religion. The way in which religion is relegated to the lumber-room of life is vividly demonstrated when we enter a modern streamlined house or a new residential quarter for office workers or for tradespeople or an industrial city which has sprung up overnight; when we get into conversation with people from such an environment, how amazed we are to discover that they are faithful Christians, in fact, one can scarcely credit the existence of Christianity at all where there isn't the slightest outward sign to indicate its existence.

The separation of life and religion is tantamount to a second Fall, a Fall occurring after the Redemption: and it is an even greater calamity than the first Fall, since not only is it a relapse but it embraces the whole of human society. We do not realise the full extent and gravity of this fall, since we too are involved and the whole atmosphere in which we live is permeated by this sin. Later ages, redeemed from this sin and able to look back on it as something past and now atoned for by the setting up of a completely new order of life and of society, will be able to measure fully the total extent of the gravity of this Fall. Unlike the sin of our First Parents, this sin was not the result of a single act, but of a mentality which gradually drifted away from God; and as a result of the gradual nature of this process, the Christian world was not even aware of its nakedness. The elements of leadership in our society were gradually lost to religion without provoking any vigorous or lasting reaction other than fruitless jeremiads about the evils of the times. And Christian society is suffering to-day the consequences of this betrayal by its leaders.

To-day we stand before the last manifestations of this separation between life and religion. We are in the unhappy position of experiencing the ills of the present epoch without foreseeing any foundations being laid for a better future. As we have said, this process of alienation of religion from life, was so gradual that it passed unperceived by a great number of people, somewhat like a light shower of ashes which gradually settled upon the field of European culture. It was only the appalling catastrophe of the First World War that revealed how far the culture of Europe had strayed from Christianity; once we had been shocked into an awareness of the position, it was then easy to trace the history of this process of secularisation. Now, anyone who fully comprehends the position cannot fail to be aware that this is a fateful moment in the history of the world and of salvation.

The separation of religion from life is more pronounced in Europe than it is in the Orient. Leaving aside the question of the Eastern religions, the Greco-Russian culture has preserved the unity of religion and life to a greater degree than in the West. The mystic element in this unity, in particular, corresponds to the spiritual organisation of Orthodox Christianity. Such things as the greater significance of the Liturgy in the life of the people, contemplative monasticism, and the way in which the everyday world is pervaded by religious symbols, even if in many cases these have become to a certain extent lifeless formalities, speak of a more intimate relationship between Christianity and cultural life. This is not necessarily to be taken as a sign of superiority on the part of the Oriental peoples; it may on the contrary be ascribed to their primitive condition, in which they have not yet experienced the tension between the two elements of religion and culture. That the West has experienced this tension first and with greater violence is due rather to the peculiar spiritual character of Western man.

The ethics of work, evolved in the Northern countries from the unremitting struggle with Nature, has a large part to play in this tension. In the more Northern countries, man had to laboriously wrest from Nature what he needed for his sustenance, and so, from the very beginning, he had to discover means of dominating Nature, by force or by fraud. Hence the more Northerly was his habitation, the more did the soul of European man take on a calculating, rationalistic element in contrast to the Eastern man, who was more passive and in greater harmony with Nature. Similarity of climate with the rest of northern Europe explains why the Russians developed a certain similarity of attitude. In their case, however, it was counter-balanced by the fact that they had received their culture from Byzantium which, in its turn, had always had its face to the East. It is clear that, in this context, economic, climatic, political and historical factors can have a great influence.

Again, the separation of religion and life is more marked in Germany than in other European countries. This is due to a great extent to the 'Enlightenment',[15] which regarded God more as the keystone of the Universe, the Prime Mover, the Transcendental or the Absolute—in these two words, abstract words, we can see the lifelessness and the coldness of such concepts of God—rather than as the immanent divine Being, present in all the operation of nature and of grace, much less still, of course, as a Saviour; and the result of this was that the godless world disintegrated into its own atoms. As well as that, there is the distinction between the 'simple clergyman' and the teacher of the sacred sciences, which hangs like a millstone around the neck of the Protestant clergy in many places to-day: this dates from Schleiermacher and Kant, who were responsible for isolating religion from all the other domains of the spiritual life, the one identifying it with sentiment and the other with morality.

The separation of religion and life has been further fostered by the modern undenominational State. Since outward religious

[15] The 'Aufklärung', or 'Enlightenment', is a phenomenon in German rationalism which appeared especially at the end of the eighteenth and the beginning of the nineteenth centuries. It purported to establish a new religion which would include no mysteries, based on the principles and dictates of natural reason penetrated with a kind of sentimental mysticism. The 'Enlightenment' wished to reconcile the differences between Protestantism and Catholicism by the establishment of a new, progressivist and universal moral system. The two great champions of truth in the face of these ideas of the 'Enlightenment' were Sailer and Moehler.

observance is impossible except under the aegis of some particular form of religion and since the various forms of religion are in themselves a source of division and of contention, the modern State, which recognises no established Church and which guarantees complete freedom of worship, is obliged to eliminate from all institutions created or fostered by it any religious character, or at any rate to dilute it as much as possible. Amongst the States of Germany, those which are predominantly Protestant have, in dealing with religious problems, done more than the Catholic States to advance this separation of religion and life, since it is more in accordance with the principles of Protestant doctrine.

The exclusion of religion from the State and municipal schools and institutes of learning has been more thoroughly effected in Germany than in other countries, notwithstanding the religious instruction given in the schools in the name of the State and the theological faculties at our Universities, of which for other reasons we are so justly proud. Another instance of the watertight barrier set up between culture and Christianity is the way in which, up to the time of the 1914-18 war, the treasures of our ancient Christian literature were rigidly excluded from classes in Old German in the secondary schools. In this context, however, we are not thinking so much of religious instruction, in so far as it is a separate school subject—though this, of course, is very important—but rather of the religious spirit and atmosphere, which should pervade all classes and all educational activity. Religion has lost its own vital character by being isolated from all other domains of the intellectual life. One pointer to this is the fact that in the schools, as well as in everyday life, religion has come to be identified with religious knowledge; and this in turn is only a parallel to the development by which education has come to be synonymous with intellectual formation, without regard to the other cultural factors, moral, artistic and religious; the natural consequence of all this is that our educational systems are geared not to true education so much as to the enrichment of the intellect, they concentrate on imparting an accumulation of knowledge and on packing the memory with all kinds of knowledge, which is often very far removed from daily life. Religion ought not to be made a subject on the curriculum, it ought also to be a spirit pervading the whole school.

It is really only now that we are beginning to feel the pinch in this matter. The teachers of religion are complaining, and rightly so, of the little time allowed for religious instruction, but a more serious matter altogether is the whole atmosphere, in which all education and instruction is enveloped; this is capable of harm which hours of religious instruction could not undo. The inferiority complex found amongst many German Catholics, even those who are of high birth, extensive possessions or outstanding scholarship, and the extraordinary degree to which they bow to the demands of the *Zeitgeist*, in comparison to people of other beliefs, can be explained only by the helplessness of their religious thinking when confronted by modern life.

Again, our public institutions in Germany are less influenced by Christianity than in most other European states. Ernst Troeltsch makes no secret of his views on this question,[16] and Max Scheler also comments: 'In no other country has a living religion failed so signally to make itself a centre of strength and unity as was the case with us in recent decades, and in no other country has the current attitude of the masses of the people towards Church and Religion been determined to such a degree by interests outside the Church as in our country.'[17]

THE FORMS OF SEPARATION

The separation as manifested in Christian culture

Religion and life are two forces, standing side by side, and both making demands on men. They form two separate worlds which are alien and hostile to each other: on the one hand there is humanism, on the other, Christianity ; on the one hand the natural goodness of man, on the other hand holiness of a religious character. In laying down this much as axiomatic, we have not yet come to any conclusions about the value either of the religious or of the cultural life. Each one, considered in itself alone, does possess a great potential value, although the very fact of their separation is an intrinsic weakness, which impedes its full development.

[16] Collected Works, Vol. 2: *Zur religiösen Lage*, Tübingen 1913, Mohr.

[17] *Christentum und Gesellschaft*, first half-volume: *Konfessionen*, Neue Geist Verlag, Leipzig, 1924, p. 140.

Culture without religion, let it be admitted straightaway, can attain to a very high level of development and can attract with magical fascination the worldly man, who nevertheless has not lost sight of all spiritual aspirations. It is just such a culture as this which Goethe portrays in his fragment 'Geheimnisse' (Mysteries) in the person of Humanus and in the articles of his manifesto. Here we find education and intelligence, nobility of soul and moral striving, the highest refinement of intellect and imagination. In such an atmosphere as this man's natural goodness and nobility can attain to its full stature. Leibnitz and Wilhelm von Humboldt, in many aspects of their lives, may be cited as products and types of this purely human culture. However, we can only point to individual figures who have approached the ideal of this pure humanity. As a universal or even widespread phenomenon, it has never existed, neither in the classic age of Greece so idealised by the humanists nor amongst the humanists themselves nor under the German Enlightenment movement. Behind the most sublime intellectualism there was concealed only too often moral laxity and insincerity in determining the norms to be followed in regard to the conduct of life, which made it only too clear that humanity, when left to its own devices and dependent on its own resources, cannot realise its ideals. Even the greatest amongst German humanists and the most distinguished figures in the movement of the Enlightenment made remarkable concessions to the lower man. And anyway, we must remember that these were only isolated figures. This highly-vaunted natural culture did not impinge on the vast mass of the people at all. The deeper insight, which modern historical and social research has given us into the life of society at the time of the Enlightenment, into the life of the courts, of the statesmen, of the ladies of nobility and of the bourgeoisie, of the students and of the ordinary folk in the streets,[18] demonstrates this with merciless clarity. And when we come to consider this purely human culture in the light of present-day conditions, it is then that we begin to feel really despondent! Frithjof Nansen assures us that it is leading us back to barbarism and Oswald Spengler sees it as doomed to decline and fall.

Looking back it is easy for us now to see that whatever its moral earnestness the Enlightenment was only an inheritance

[18] Cf. Wilhelm Lütgert, *Die Religion des deutschen Idealismus und ihr Ende*, Part I, Gütersloh 1923, K. Bertelsmann, pp. 220–272.

from the greater Christian past. Since then this inheritance has been almost entirely used up and hence our moral bankruptcy is becoming more and more apparent. That the culture of our times has been able to put up such a splendid front for so long and to dazzle the eye of the beholder with its wonders was due to its aesthetic and technical brilliance rather than to any ethical or social content. It is true that even to-day a purely human culture, divorced from Christianity, can point to great figures and to relatively great achievements, but they are very few, due to the fact that the name of God or of Christ is excluded by this kind of culture or at any rate does not play a fundamental part in its thinking. St. Augustine had the same experience with the Manichaeans, saying that even though they invoked the beautiful name of Truth in their discourses and in their countless books, the name of the Eternal Truth was missing from their philosophy.[19]

On the other side stands Christianity. This, too, is a mighty and highly developed power, especially in what pertains to the inner life of the Church. It is a power which is conscious of its own strength, which has a promise of certain endurance and which makes great demands on the whole man, entire and undivided. It has produced great saints, who can evoke admiration from even the most worldly. It has used not only the old methods but also the best modern methods to fashion a science of Theology; it has founded an asceticism, which can make men saints; in its legal code it has provided for all the Christian communal and personal relationships and brought them into harmony with the central unity of the Church; and it has fostered a liturgy, than which no better expression of collective piety exists.

But this Christianity is living for the most part in a ghetto, and life seems to be passing over its head. It is far from being the leaven which should permeate humanity and human relationships and make them pleasing to God. Science and morality, economy and trade, the private and public life of society pay little or even no heed to Christianity and to its dictates. This ghetto condition is all the more deplorable when it is not enforced on Christianity by those who are leaders in cultural matters but is actually freely adopted by the Christians themselves, who resign themselves to this condition or who even are quite content with it and glad not to be obliged to take upon themselves the task of solving the world's ills. They

[19] Confessions III, 6.

may allow themselves to sink into this ghetto condition either
because they really don't think the ills of the world are as
black as they are painted, or because they feel there is nothing
they can do about it, or because they feel that even if they
were to try to do something about it, the world would not take
them seriously.

Now this ghetto condition affects not only Christianity as a
whole but Catholicism in particular, and that holds for German
Catholicism as well. If we go very deeply into the reasons for
this state of affairs, we are faced once again with the early
Christian attitude to the Parousia, or Second Coming, from
which Christianity has never, since the departure of its Founder,
been able to shake itself quite free. The German is, of all
peoples, the one who is most given to system and method—
whatever he does or does not do, all must be in accordance
with some basic principle or system. In the case of other peoples,
for instance the Latins and the English, a healthy illogicality
kept them from completely severing the bonds which they
found existing between religion and life. But in any conflict
between science and faith, the German, with that excessive
reliance on reason and logic which is peculiar to his national
character, tends to have greater confidence in the former.
For instance, it has been pointed out that in the conflict
between religion and evolution, the source of so much passionate
controversy, the German tended to favour the latter position,
whereas the educated American tended to take the side of
religion.[20]

In considering this matter of the attitude of German
Catholicism, which is most strongly entrenched in the Rhineland, to the duty of tackling the cultural problems of the nation,
we must remember how unfortunate it was that, after the
French Revolution, the State looked with mistrust and
malevolence on the newly-formed Catholic states, and even
burst into open hostility in the 'Kölner Wirren' of the years
after 1837 and in the 'Kulturkampf'. This had a twofold
effect: on the one hand, the State and its official organs
took up a more rigid and hostile attitude to Catholicism,
cutting itself off from any beneficial influences which might
have been forthcoming from that quarter; on the other hand,
large sections of the Catholic population were led to regard

[20] *Entwicklungslehre und Religion*, von Bavink: Review '*Unsere
Welt*', published by the Keplerbund of Detmold, XV, Febr. 1924,
p. 25.

4

the State as the natural enemy, and since the State came to be seen more and more as the administrator and the caretaker of the cultural possessions of the nation, the Catholics came to lose any influence on, or interest in, the cultural life of the nation, as had already been their fate in regard to its political life. Those citizens and statesmen, who were active in the Rhineland areas, were so preoccupied for such a long period of time in fighting a retreat on the politico-ecclesiastical front that they were not able to give themselves to the work of fostering cultural values with that tranquility, which alone brings success in this field. This conflict and its consequences led to religion being regarded not so much as a means of spiritual renovation as a source of political influence. 'During the Kulturkampf they looked on Catholicism as a rampart which had to be defended, a city of God, and during this defence they had no time to observe the quiet inner growth of Catholicism or to give expression to that growth in works which would be congenial to its spirit.'[21] As far as ecclesiastical matters and the interior life is concerned German Catholicism compares well with that of any other country; but its influence on life in general, on science, literature, art, social and economic matters, falls below that of most other European countries, even in those where ecclesiastical and spiritual life seems less strong and in those where the Church has less influence in politics than it has with us.

The separation as manifested in the individual

The same dichotomy, which is evident in the general picture of religion and life, is seen repeated to a greater depth in the individual man. In him, religion and life exist side by side; the one and the same man is at one moment a man of this world, at the next a Christian. At his prayer he gives himself to God, in his work he takes back the gift again. Even convinced Christians are apt to resemble in their business dealings that Roman legionary, who besought the god Hermes that a looting operation might be successful for him, so that, he might bring a sacrifice to Zeus from the booty. Outside the precincts of the church, the Christian can scarcely be distinguished from the non-Christian. The norms by which they allow themselves to be guided in marriage, in business and

[21] Max Scheler, *Christentum und Gesellschaft*, Leipzig, Verlag der Neue Geist, first half-vol. 1924 p. 148.

their social lives, are, by and large, essentially the same. If a man were really to be formed by Christianity, it should be possible to tell at first glance whether he were a Christian or a non-Christian. But to-day religion is not something vital like the life-blood flowing through the veins; the term divine worship, for instance, is kept completely apart from daily work and life, and is confined solely to the sacred functions which are carried out in church. To God we owe prayer and divine worship, to the world we have other duties to perform, whereas our whole lives should in reality be one continuous prayer before God. The full import of the words of St. John about spiritual rebirth and new life, the words of St. Paul about the new creation and of St. Peter about our participation in the divine nature, are scarcely comprehended any longer. Man is, as it were, leading a double life and so a grotesque element of duplicity and insincerity is being introduced into his life.

The external sign of the destruction of the equilibrium between religion and life is a distortion both of the religious life and of cultural activity, never witnessed in normal times. Cut adrift from life, religion can acquire a character of strangeness or eccentricity, descending even to the level of caricature, which can be a source of scandal to healthy piety and of cheap mockery to the impious. On the other hand, social life, when not ultimately bound up with religion, tends to lose sight of higher ideals and to lapse into melancholy and boredom or even to wallow in the deceptive pleasures of this world. The incapacity for straight thinking on moral or religious ideas, found to-day even in the most cultivated circles, is only an external symptom of the spiritual degeneracy of those who have lost sight of the intimate bond between religion and life and who think they are living, when, in reality, they are merely vegetating. They give social worship to God without any inner piety, their system of law ignores moral factors and justice has no place in matters of trade and economy; in short, all those values which are axiomatic to the natural right-thinking man are disregarded.

The fact of this separation of religion and life is a particularly painful one for us. On the one hand, we are caught up in the flowing tide of the culture of our own people and our own age, and our love for our nation and its culture are such that we do not wish to find fault with it. Such is our pride in Nature, Art, History, in the Fatherland, in short, in life itself in all its varying forms and appearances, and such is our awareness of cultural values that we would be loth to cut ourselves adrift from this culture or to belong to a culturally backward society. On the other hand Religion and Church are for us vital matters, which concern not only the heart but the whole man, and which are of vital importance to us. Any man who has once understood the idea of the fatherhood of God can never abandon his Creator, nor can he ever forget the face of Jesus once he has beheld it; a man who has realised what it means to be a member of the Communion of Saints can never find satisfaction outside it. To the religious man, a world without God is only a desert; a life in which Christ has no part would not be worth living and a life outside the Church would be for him an exile. Thus it is that our nature is torn between these two forces which are at war with each other; this is what makes our situation so difficult. If a man is not to be torn apart in the struggle, it would appear that he must yield to one of the opposing forces.

And in fact, the separation of religion and life has gradually led to a false and one-sided idea of both. The mundane man sees Christianity as something which is essentially remote from the world and hostile to it and its culture; for him the only true embodiment of the religious ideal is the hermit who withdraws into the desert and retires altogether from the world, and the fact that all pious people do not adopt this way of life he sees as a sort of dispensation or perhaps even as a concession to human frailty. To most people the saint as a representative of the religious ideal in all its purity becomes a kind of unreal fantasy, without flesh and blood or any human likelihood. On the other hand, a purely human culture, however noble, is not justly appreciated by religious people. For them, all cultural strivings are mere folly and vanity, science is regarded as a danger to faith, preoccupation with the values of this world leads to the service of the world, and active participation in civic or cultural life can only lead to conflict with the Church or with religion.

We see, then, that this state of conflict between two forces, each of which is trying to win the individual man for itself, can become a barrier to faith for the one man, who, in a positivistic frame of mind, tries to examine and assess the effectiveness and influence of the Church and of Christianity, and for another man can become a barrier to life, in so far as he looks upon the goods of this world from the purely spiritual point of view and hence can no longer come to terms with the world. The one loses his faith for the sake of the world, the other the world for the sake of faith.

The harm caused to both religion and life

In the physical order, when things which belong together are torn apart with violence, then a wound is caused, which can be fatal for both sides. But in moral organisms the damage done goes beyond the mere fact of separation; an element of alienation and hostility between the parts is introduced. When Schleiermacher, for instance, wrote his *Discourses on Religion*, he did not direct them against the cultured who were indifferent to religion, but against 'those cultured, who despise religion.' This separation of religion and life is harmful to cultural life. Culture is, of itself, an incomplete thing, lacking a final unity, since it excludes not only a most basic and essential factor in human nature but also the highest of all cultural values. It fails to fulfil the greatest and most noble needs of the human soul, which is essentially and naturally Christian. The Church's ideal of christianising all human relationships is reflected in the blessings and consecrations which she makes available for things in profane use, not only for house and field, man and beast, but also for such things as means of trade and communication, ships, bridges and railways and even for the telegraph; in these blessings the earthly things become for her a symbol of something heavenly. These blessings and the spirit which inspires them are almost unknown to the modern man, a clear indication that he has lost all feeling for such religious symbolism.

At a meeting of a Trade Union council some time ago, a religiously disposed foreman said that he saw no reason why the Church should not have or introduce a special blessing for the modern factory and its machines. The thing is, however, that the Church has such blessings, as we see from its liturgical books[22] but they are never requested. Our modern industrial life has no longer any time for that sort of thing. And many smile at the idea that to-day in Spain things of a definitely profane and perhaps even morally questionable character, such as races and bullfights, are sometimes inaugurated by a religious

[22] Cf. the manuals of popular Liturgy edited by the Abbey of Maria Laach, XI, Freiburg, Herder.

ceremony; but they fail to understand the motive underlying this.

The German, the most methodical of men, has gone all the way in his secularisation of private and public life. The naturally noble man, who has never known or possessed religion, is like a torso; following this image, the man who has lost religion is like a mutilated statue. Culture, divorced from religion, is culture without a soul. The thinking man cannot continue to live like this; either his sense of religion will become atrophied altogether or one day he will make the same discovery as did St. Augustine, who summed up the results of a long and tortuous search through all systems of philosophy and theology in the words: 'Thou has made us for thyself, O God, and our heart will never rest until it rests in thee'.

The exclusion of the religious element from cultural life must of necessity leave a void; for religion just as much as speech or culture belongs to the totality of human nature. This void is genuinely felt and so the soul seeks more or less consciously for some values to fill it. The great desire seen amongst our people of making themselves acquainted with the fruits of scientific scholarship by availing of adult education, lecture courses, and literary evenings, all stems from the 'hope, which one is often not aware of or does not like to admit, of freeing oneself from spiritual gnawings and from the disquiet and tedium of life by the satisfaction of intellectual desires.'[23] And when science and all other means fail to fill this void, then the religious factor is preserved but generally applied to some false object. In place of religion one has an unsound mysticism, in the place of God, an idol. Where there is no faith, there must be superstition and where God is not, then spirits rule. Such things as Theosophy and Anthroposophy, occultism and spiritism rise up out of the ruins of religion. Again the hatred of the proletariat for religion and church is proof that, in the religious sphere, neutrality is impossible. Even with the much-vaunted and in fact considerable religious and civic tolerance of Liberalism, which is indifferent to religion and church, it does not require much to fan aflame another 'Kulturkampf'.

When Cagliostro, the trickster, wonder-worker and conjurer of evil spirits, was condemned to lifelong imprisonment by the Papal Inquisition, Goethe wrote to Jacobi as follows: 'It is

[23] Arthur Liebert, *Die geistige Krisis der Gegenwart*, Berlin 1923, Pan, Rolf Heise, p. 198.

painful to see how people cry out for wonders, with the sole result of remaining so sunk in their own folly and stupidity, that
they reject and defy the supreme seat of human intelligence
and reason.'[24] It is the representatives of industry and of the
wealthy who are most eager for these substitutes for religion;
and this is further proof of how little the culture of this earth is
designed to appease the spiritual hunger of man, destined for
immortality. Culture alone cannot fulfil man's needs and so
cannot make him happy, and it is a remarkable fact that after
a period of climax in purely human culture there is always a
period of cultural pessimism: that this should be so is no
accident but a consequence of the intrinsic nature of the human
soul. Mankind has never been so discontented, so starved of
love and so far from true happiness as in the recent past, an
age whose culture was so much extolled. But the voices
glorifying this great age of culture have become more subdued
in recent times, and it appears that humanity is now beginning
to realise just how much it is missing and to take stock of the
real situation.

The separation is harmful also for religion. Religion is the
right relation of man to God, and so it addresses itself to the
whole man, just as life also claims the whole man. Religion
seeks to rule man in all his energies and purposes, as well as
in all his human relationships. It is not just one aspect of the
life of the spirit, nor is it something confined to one faculty of
the soul; neither is it merely a higher level in the general
culture of the human spirit. Religion is incomplete without
culture. It seeks to pervade all human relationships; it does
not build on nature as on a foundation, but raises it up and
realises its true being. Even in the more fortunate position,
where religion is still felt as a great interior force, the separation
of religion and worldly culture is a great tragedy; the blood-
stream of religion is choked and cut off, and it becomes a foreign
element in the midst of life. How far this process has gone is
shown by the inability of our religious leaders or leading circles
to exert any influence in the burning questions of our day, as
for instance, questions of social or moral import, questions of
marriage, family, education, physical culture and the great
issue of world peace. It is as if religion had lost its power to
revitalise the world, as if it were no longer catholic, that is to
say, embracing all human conditions and problems. And again,

[24] Quoted in Wilhelm Lütgert, *Die Religion des deutschen Idealismus
und ihr Ende*, I 217.

pastoral resources and methods must necessarily fail in the face of this separation from the world, since the man of to-day is bound too closely to the world.

The harm done is greater still, however, when religion is understood and practised as something merely external. Then the religious life becomes a lie, and religion and church are in the nature of foreign bodies, which are intrinsically at variance with the organism within which they are placed. The alien attitude of many religious men and circles in regard to nature and to life, their lack of initiative and independence in taking up an attitude to new problems, their uncritical assessment of literary figures and achievements, their inability to appreciate the point of view of anyone who differs from them: all these are the fruits of the exclusion of every religious element from the panorama of life. The phenomenon, much observed among religious people, that their attitude in religious matters is not in conformity with their attitude to the conduct of life, contributes to some extent to the lack of understanding with which non-religious men judge and treat religion, whether Catholic or Protestant, and to the fact that, in almost every country, Catholics, even when they are in the majority, are confounded by non-christians or members of other faiths who are better acquainted with nature and more in touch with the natural and profane elements in the world, elements unknown to or shunned by the Catholic. Hence it has come to pass that religion, which should govern all regions of human culture, has to occupy an attic in the great edifice of European culture and, what is worse, it seems to content itself with this poor lodging.

This separation from life leaves religion not only incomplete but also internally weakened. As with a physical organism, when the life retires into the innermost cells then the outer cells wither up and die away, so too with religion. When religion ceases to animate the whole man in his several relationships to life, then authority and law must impress themselves with a deeper weight as a result of the loss of complete spiritual freedom entailed. When the spirit of faith and of prayer does not surge outwards, transforming the whole christian life into worship of God, then some practical exercises will be needed to supplant this defect and to maintain at least an exterior contact with the spirit.

Here again, we have a strange and tragic paradox, from which there seems to be no escape! The weaker the interior spiritual life of any man, class or age becomes, the more must the Church employ law and prohibition to conserve this 'vita minima', so that the vital principle of this life may not die out altogether: 'Do not touch, nor taste, nor handle!'[25] Again, the less equipped the divine life, which exists in the soul, to confront the culture of the world, the less vigorous does that divine life become, and the weaker its possible influence on human affairs.[26]

The religious man of to-day is too weak to put up a fight, and he is getting weaker all the time, because he is losing heart for the fight. It is a terrible dilemma, which we might express by saying that the man of to-day is like one who has not attained his majority. The Church cannot declare him to be of age, because he is not so, and yet he cannot come of age, because the Church cannot declare him to be so. 'For to everyone that hath shall be given, and he shall abound: but from him that hath not, that also which he seemeth to have shall be taken away.'[27] Yet in this withdrawal of the life of the spirit into the innermost recesses of the soul, there may be a Providential design, in as much as life is preserved until it can burst forth under more favourable external circumstances.

The condition of tension, then, which should exist between religion and life, and which should be a law of life and of progress, has become a condition of separation and this separation has become an almost universally acknowledged fact. One could be tempted to use the lamentation of the prophet Jeremias[28] in reference to European culture: 'How doth the city sit solitary, that was full of people! How is the mistress of the Gentiles become as a widow, the princess of provinces made tributary!' It is necessary that we see the distress of our

---

[25] Colossians 2, 21.

[26] In this connection there arises a pressing practical problem. Authority, in every sphere, desires to help liberty, as yet imperfect, to perfect itself, and must do so, if it understands its mission correctly; yet it cannot permit any violation of order, even where that violation is purely material. Therefore, contrary to its original purpose of freeing man and giving him a chance to perfect himself, it must set up laws and restrictions, which may have the effect of depriving the one who is to be freed of some of the freedom which he already enjoys. This is an apparent contradiction, for which there is no satisfactory theoretical answer; we can only arrive at a practical solution. 'The human spirit comes to maturity, from the point of view of reason, only by its own efforts, which it must be free to make', says Kant in Die Religion, etc., ed. Karl Kehrbach, Leipzig, in Reclam series, note to page 204.

[27] Matthew 25, 29.

[28] Lamentations 1, 1.

situation, not merely so as to be distressed, but to be distressed to the point of repentance, a distress which will be pleasing to God, for in the words of St. Paul, 'the sorrow that is according to God worketh penance, steadfast unto salvation; but the sorrow of the world worketh death.'[29] *We must emerge from the ghetto,* we must remove the state of hostility which exists between the Church and the culture of the world! We must return from the exile into which we have been banished, or rather, freely gone! The motto, 'Down from the Tower', even though coined by the political representatives of Catholicism, holds good to-day also for the whole domain of culture among Catholic people.

A genuine man and a genuine culture cannot continue to live such a double life for a very long time. 'No man can serve two masters.' We are now at the parting of the ways, and we must go one way or the other, unless we can find a way of uniting the two forms of life, the christian and the purely cultural. If religion remains divorced from life, then it will soon become a mere form of orthodox ritualism, and if the culture of the world remains alien to religion, then it, in turn, will soon become mere civilisation. The two forms, of course, will remain as they are for some time to come, like a beautiful corpse or the façade of an abandoned palace. In fact, it could even happen that the Church and religion, though cut away from the world, could present a delusive appearance of splendid flowering, particularly as regards outward organisation and religious sanctions, like a candle which bursts into one last flame, giving the illusion of brightness, and then dies away; and it may also happen that profane culture will produce a certain weak nobility, which the jaded palate will find pleasing, but which will be lacking in vigour and the promise of life and will be only the forerunner of decay.

[29] II Corinthians 7, 9.

3
The effect
on Christian culture

The consequence of this separation has been the arrival of new divisions within life itself and within religion; a consequence more fateful for religion and life than for the human being who is complete in himself. When religion and life are now no longer interwoven with one another, then the inner bonds, which keep each one together, begin to lose their grip. Religion splits up, as does life, into new divisions and a process of disintegration sets in, such that it is very hard to see where it will ultimately end unless in the destruction of culture and Christianity alike. To-day there is nowhere to be found an intelligence capable of assimilating all the culture of the age and giving it a personal interpretation, as was the case with Aristotle, Albert the Great and even Leibnitz; and this is due not only to the tremendous differentiation which has since their day arisen in the sciences and in cultural life, but also in the divergence between the different domains of culture, which ceased to be a unity with the disappearance of that relation of tension between them and that unified system of philosophical and religious thinking, which kept them in a state of perfect equilibrium.

DIVISIONS WITHIN THE RELIGIOUS SPHERE

False Concepts of religion

Within the sphere of religion divergencies are cropping up, which are contrary to the nature of religion and which penetrate

to the very heart of the matter. The subject of religion is the
whole man. Religion is the right ordering of man to God,
ordo hominis ad Deum, as St. Thomas defined it, combining
simplicity with depth; the subject of religion, therefore, is
the whole psycho-physical essence of man, and not just the
soul or any of the faculties. In this matter, rationalism has
torn apart things which form a biological unity and has given
the parts an independent existence. But the nature of man is
a unity, which must be taken all together. If, however, it is to
be methodically dissected, this must be on the understanding
that it is not something natural but rather a means towards
an end. These means lead to knowledge, but have as little
independent existence as the tracks of a caravan in the desert
sands. It is the whole man, then, and not such parts as may
be arrived at by this process of analysis and dissection, who is
the sole subject of religion and religious action. Just as the life
of Jesus cannot really be analysed by historical criticism but
must be understood as a whole, so too religion cannot be
understood as merely one aspect of the life of the spirit.

As a consequence of the divisions of which we have been
speaking, different faculties of the soul are variously cited as
the subject of religion. In the first place, we have the religion
of the intelligence or of culture, that is to say, the religion of
the Aufklärung, or Enlightenment. According to this, faith in
God is needed to complete our picture of the world and to explain terrestrial phenomena; but it offers as little room for a
warm loving relationship between God and man as it does for
a God who condescends to grant grace to man. The fearfulness
and helplessness of many believing Christians, even among
those who are schooled in theology, when confronted with new
problems, and their excessive horror of research, is not always
based on well-founded mistrust of reason in the dangerous
heights of theological speculation, but is based to a great
extent on the conviction that faith is a concern of the intelligence. It would follow from this that every new intellectual
change of position in regard to the faith would be also a change
of faith.

Then again, religion is made a concern of the will and of
the moral order. As in the view of Kant, religion is equivalent
to morality. Religion is 'to know our duties as divine commands', and is distinguished from morality itself only in so far
as the dictates of the law-giving practical reason are seen to
be at the same time the commands of a supreme Being. Thus

religion becomes a sort of appendix to morality, as if God could be known only by means of the categorical imperative. It is a widespread idea that the essence of religion consists in being an honourable man, and the many societies for ethical culture, which cultivate morality for its own sake, start off from this fundamental presupposition.

For others religion is a feeling or sentiment, the consciousness of our smallness and nothingness in the face of the Universe, 'a feeling for and a taste for the infinite', in the words of Schleiermacher. It is the religion of the beautiful soul. There is a vague misty quality about it, setting such store as it does by the ecstatic delight in the mysterious, the delicious thrill of fear in the face of the infinite, the delirium of tender devotion. Practical piety, it may be added, has taken to itself something of this religious sentiment, which is the creation of natures of extremely heightened sensibilities or endowed with mystical gifts. Or again in the pragmatic conception of religion, it is one of the values of life. The watchword of this view is 'Oh well, one must have religion' or 'Religion must be preserved for the sake of the people', or 'If there weren't such a thing as religion, it would have to be invented', for the sake of the mob, that is, who could not otherwise be held in check. This has sometimes been called the American conception of religion, which can be expressed in the following formula: religion is true if it works, and in so far as it works; the converse, however, is not true, that it works because it is true.

The view is widely current that religion is an affair for the individual man, but not for communities of men, 'Religion is a private matter', and so family, state and society, as such, fall outside its radius. It is this view which leads to the demand for the separation of Church and state, religion and the schools. Now while a community is a moral unity, the individual is a very complex organism—*individuum est ineffabile*—and so the religious interests of the individual are limitless in number and variety of content. Hence this individualism begets a selfish streak even in the midst of piety. The lapidary style of prayer born of community worship, in which everything centres upon the kingdom of God, gives place to an individualistic piety, which finds expression in countless devotional exercises and petty selfish prayers of petition. The 'we' style becomes the 'I' style in prayer and hymn. The sense of the Eucharist as a communal repast is lost or watered down, and even our general communions, that is, communal participation in the Eucharistic Banquet, no longer denote a clear community sense.

Finally we have the exaggerated view of religion as something purely interior; religion becomes solely a concern of the soul and is practised in the silence of the heart, requiring neither temple, nor worship in common. The Church is an invisible church, known only to the eyes of God; sacrament, sacrifice and liturgy do not belong to the essence of religion.

We even hear the view, which brings us down to the level of the trivial and the frivolous, that religion is something for women and children but not for strong manly spirits; or something for the old but not for exuberant youth; or something for times of need, which can be forgotten in times of good fortune.

It is easy to realise how each one of these ideas sacrifices the true essence of religion. Each one contains some germ of truth but not the whole truth, and each one takes the streams of religious vitality and channels them into one narrow outlet, so that they cannot break free to fall on the plains of life and make them fruitful. The words of St. Paul give a different picture altogether: 'For the word of God is living and effectual and more piercing than any two-edged sword, and reaching unto the division of soul and the spirit, of the joints also and the marrow; and is a discerner of the thoughts and intents of the heart.'[1]

The concept of the Church

The way in which the very nature of religion is made narrower and falsified, as we have outlined above, must necessarily lead to changing views on the effects and operations of religion in the world. When the subject of religion becomes not the whole man but some part or aspect of man, then its value and effectiveness are limited also and violence is done to the broad Christian and Catholic concept of religion.

For one thing, the Church is reduced to a mere religious confession. But true religion cannot possibly become a mere creed. Concerning the whole man, as such, *catholicity* is a necessary feature of it. Since to be a Christian is to be a child of God, and since all men are called to be children of God, then it follows that there can be no division in the religious society based on different ages, cultures, races or social classes.

[1] Hebrews 4, 12.

Fundamentally, therefore, any watering down of the idea of religion leads to a destruction of religion itself in some way and to some extent; yet the fact is that in the religious society of our time the *idea* of religion has been corrupted and religion has accordingly been affected also. For many the word 'catholic' has lost its religious significance and warmth, and has taken on a sense of something partisan and controversial. When men limit themselves to membership of a particular persuasion, either because of complacent satisfaction with that confession or because of fear to come in contact with those outside it, then there is a resultant impoverishment in spiritual values, and the process of divinising the culture of the world is slowed up.

The division of European Christendom into confessions is regarded by many as a tragedy which has now firmly established itself and must be accepted as a *fait accompli*; the most they will do is to occasionally express a wish that it may one day please Providence to heal this division in some miraculous way instead of being really distressed at seeing the Body of Christ dismembered in this way and racking their brains to devise means to lead the daughter of Sion back from exile. In the Catholic Church, unity of faith is guaranteed by its constitution, but outside the Church, religious individualism could and did, push itself to its most extreme limits.

The Church, however, is a community, which embraces all times, cultures, nations, classes and ranks of society; it is above all distinction of time and culture, above all distinction of class and profession, and above all nationalism. It does not exclude anything which exists and has a positive value. 'For there is no man that doth a miracle in my name and can soon speak ill of me. For he that is not against you, is for you',[2] says the Master. But anyone can shut himself off from the Church by choosing some religious values and doctrines and rejecting others, that is to say, by heresy. The only one who is declared by the Church to be cut off in this way is the man who cuts himself off by this uncatholic particularism.

This narrowing of the idea of the Church and the way in which the confessions set up boundaries against one another has its effect in the defensive attitude adopted by many clergymen in the training of the souls committed to their care. Their only thought is to defend them against the world, rather than to equip them for the world. Now the modern world is so evil and

[2] Mark 9, 38 f.

so corrupt that it is necessary to defend them, but since most men are obliged to take their places in the midst of the world, the best way to defend and preserve their religious and moral principles is to teach them to defeat evil by good and to be able to hand on this training to others. This is a more positive and therefore a more difficult task than the former, but circumstances indicate its necessity.

In addition, it is not only Catholicism which hides itself away in a ghetto as, whether they care to admit it or not, the Protestants are in a ghetto also, inasmuch as that they shut themselves off from any contact with Catholicism or Catholic culture. Indeed, they often seal themselves off so hermetically that it is possible for them to have completely false notions of Catholic doctrine and morals even while they are conducting elaborate scientific investigations into strange religions, and that the gross prejudices which they entertain cannot be overcome by even the most frequent external contact.[3]

A further sign of the division within religion is religious nationalism. And here we see reflected in the relationship of peoples and nations to one another what is also to be observed in mutual relations of individual men. Men are more conscious of the relation between God and the individual soul than they are of the relation between God and society; and the oft-heard phrase about a man taking counsel with 'his' God has deeper implications than might appear at first sight. Now, just as a man will speak of 'his' God, so too nations are apt to claim God or also certain saints as their own, though it is not at all clear what such expressions mean in regard to the nations' idea of God, even when they are seriously meant.

Again, in this regard, we must remember the fundamental opposition between the romano-celtic and germanic peoples, even within the Church. In spite of the continual struggles between Papacy and Empire, the Middle Ages did have a strong consciousness of Catholic unity; and the consciousness of this unity in the early centuries of the Church is brought home to us by the fact that an Oriental could be bishop in a city of the West and vice versa. Can we imagine to-day a priest of Cologne becoming bishop of Paris or a Belgian being bishop

[3] Heinrich Hermelink, *Katholizismus und Protestantismus der Gegenwart*, Gotha-Stuttgart, Fr. A. Perthes, p. 50.

Friedrich Thimme, *Vom innern Frieden des deutschen Volkes*, a book for the promotion of mutual trust and understanding[2], Leipzig 1916, S. Hirzel, p. 131–136.

of Munich, even though all these places are in the same Continent! It has been said, not unwisely, that the first heresy, which the next Ecumenical Council of the Church will have to deal with, is the modern heresy of nationalism. That Catholicism in one country can come to blows with Catholicism in another is a symptom of a deep division and shows that the souls of the nations are more united by human blood than by the divine Blood of the Eucharist, and that national pride and selfishness have gained the upper hand over the spirit of religion. It is mortifying to recall that it was the Socialists and the Free- masons, not Christians, who after the First World War took the first steps towards bridging the gap between the nations. Again in this respect, there are already signs of improvement, though it is as yet only in the hands of the few; but these few are the best amongst the nations and the most faithful children of the Church.

The gap between the clergy and the laity has been widened to an extreme degree. One outward sign of this is the way in which Theology has cut itself off from the other sciences and in which theologians have cut themselves off from other scholars, and vice versa. Now it is true that there must be some degree of division between clergy and laity in a community which is, at the same time, a hierarchical society; because a community, which is entrusted with the protection and con- servation of a divine truth and a divine life, needs some deposit to guard this inheritance and needs some final authority, which is capable of speaking with divine authority in vital questions. Hence Jesus was only acting as was required by the nature of a religious society, when he chose disciples from amongst the members of his church and chose apostles from amongst these disciples and finally from amongst the apostles chose one to be their head.

This hierarchical distinction does not mean humiliation for the laity, as Kant asserted; and indeed, such could hardly be the case if, as was the Master's will, a different law ruled in the kingdom of God than in worldly spheres, namely, a law by which the greater is become as the lesser and the master as the slave, and the clergy, following the model of the Son of Man, is not come to be ministered unto but to minister. But what is humiliating to the laity is to see all responsibility and care for the kingdom of God left to the priesthood, due to their own indolence, and to see that outside of the clergy the only ones who are entrusted any longer with any share in helping the priest in the exercise of his priestly office are little boys.

Besides the official priesthood of the Church, which is separated for that purpose, there is also the universal priesthood, but of this we have in large measure lost sight. No right-thinking man will deny that the priest is of great importance as a pastor and leader of souls, he must be the 'form of the flock'; however, it is towards spiritual adulthood that he must lead them. The final goal of all education, even though it may never be attained, is to make the one who is being taught independent. In recent times efforts are being made to re-establish the lay apostolate in various forms, yet the gap between the clergy and the laity is still too great. In saying this, we do not mean to assert that the clergy is shutting itself off from the people and has no sympathy with its social needs, quite the contrary, in fact.

The German clergy at least has always had the reputation not only of having faced up to social problems at a time when other christian circles were not even concerned about them— not only that, but also of having attacked them vigorously and contributed greatly to their solution. What is in question here is rather an excessive gap between clergy and laity in religious matters. It is as if the clergy alone made up the Church and as if there were laid upon them alone, in virtue of their office, the entire responsibility for the coming of the kingdom of God on earth. It is not without significance that St. Paul, the disciple of the Pharisees who had been freed from the yoke of the synagogue, chose from out the vast treasurehouse of the Greek speech the beautiful word *ecclesia* to describe what has been created by Jesus Christ. For *ecclesia*, following the traditional meaning of the word, means the assembled community or more exactly the assembly of the communities, and not just the Pope or the bishops or the hierarchy of the Church. Each and every member of this *ecclesia* is responsible for its destiny and must contribute to shaping and bringing about the coming of the kingdom of God on this earth.

It is due to the division between religion and life that in the religious affairs of the community the laity leave the field to the clergy as a general rule. It was a different story altogether in the days of the early Church, when without prejudice to devout reverence and in willing subordination to authority, even the ordinations took place with the approval of the whole church, 'consentiente universa ecclesia.'[4] At the time, the Church, in the minds of the faithful, was the community of all those who had been sanctified by Baptism, and not just the teaching Church. It is like the words of Jesus, when he said that the Sabbath was made for man, not man for the Sabbath.[5]

To-day, the laity does not have an opinion in matters which affect the church and religion, more as a result of indifference than fear or reverence for the clergy, Now, it is not solely the women who are 'keeping silent in the assembly', which is their duty and right, it being only fitting that they, as the mystic principle in all piety, should maintain a devout silence during the divine worship, but the men also are keeping silent. All questions of christian culture are left to the Church, and cooperation is only forthcoming when requested. It is only a half-hearted cooperation at that. How seldom it happens that the laity, acting from an acute understanding of the spiritual needs of the times, make a scientific foundation or set up a religious society or come together to discuss matters of interest to Catholic culture, unless they are encouraged to do so by spiritual or ecclesiastical authorities! And the first steps in Catholic Action, the initiative in the institution of new church feasts or canonisations, even when they have reference to a particular country or a particular profession, for instance, a feast of 'Jesus the Worker', are seldom taken by the competent lay circles. The attitude is that the Church must look after itself, as if Catholics had no responsibility for the destiny of God's kingdom on earth, of which they are citizens. The Middle Ages had a much more heightened sense of the obligation of the laity to cooperate in spiritual tasks and of the solidarity which should bind the spiritual and mundane interests.

Closely related to what we have been saying is the fact that the Church's failure to exercise any lasting influence on public and social life is due largely to the lack of any popular character in the Church's present-day life and action. The majority of baptised people to-day, even baptised Catholics, especially in the cities, no longer belong interiorly to the society of the Church. If they take any part in religious life, it is only a purely exterior one. The Church offers its treasures, but they are despised: she preaches but no one listens. And even among those who listen, the Word of God often strikes no spark in their souls. The words of a city adolescent, 'It's so funny to

[4] St. Clement of Rome, *Letter to the Corinthians* 44, 3.
[5] St. Mark 2, 27.

see a church right in the middle of Berlin' show just how much
influence religious instruction has on the greater part of our
city youth. Man belongs principally to this life—as the saying
has it, he must be born before he is reborn. Hence the immediate, the tangible, the visible has for him the greater attraction.
True, he recognises that religion is also a factor in life; but what
is he to do, when the two seem to be in conflict with one another?
One must yield place to the other, unless he is to serve now the
one and now the other, as so often happens, and end up by
serving neither. Normally, however, the more immediate and
tangible thing will have the greater power to attract, and so
religion falls silently into the background; it becomes lifeless,
and a certain force is then needed to wrench it from its passive
state. Catholicism has had reason to be ashamed that, until
recently, its scientific research, even in the realms of theology,
was undertaken by non-Catholics, who also brought to light
the treasures of our christian past in liturgy, mysticism,
hagiography and folklore, and nourished themselves upon them.
In this way they presented Catholicism to the world as a
religious phenomenon, while we did not bestir ourselves to
present it as a form of life, much less to live that form of life.

Another significant fact is that learned Catholic societies,
as for instance the *Görres-Gesellschaft*, have a membership
mainly of theologians and could hardly survive without the
support of the clergy. Yet another outward symbol of the way
in which the religious element in modern man lacks vitality and
naturalness is the unproductivity of our age in everything
relating to liturgy, sacred music and ecclesiastical architecture.
Christianity now has to be content with a more or less enthusiastic imitation of older forms. We might also point to
the pathetic persuasiveness resorted to by sacred eloquence
to-day, in order to put across the truths of faith; how it contrasts with the unadorned sobriety of the teaching of Jesus
and with the refreshing simplicity of the homilies of the ancient
Fathers. That the homilies of the Fathers could be so plain
and simple is easy to understand. The people were full of holy
fervour and it needed only a spark to fan it into flame. To-day
the picture is different! The excessive subtlety of method and
refinement of techniques which must be resorted to in religious
instruction and in all the varied works of the parish in order
to awaken interest in a matter which should be of concern to
every right-thinking soul, the unwearying organisation and
reorganisation necessary to bring some religious influence to

bear on men, already organised into the community of the Catholic Church. All these stem from the intuitive realisation on the part of Christians and of their religious leaders that the religious domain has somehow been cut adrift from the life around it, and that the Christian must be subjected to the most persuasive eloquence and the most insistent urgings to keep him in the fold.

The Germans are admitted to be masters of organisation, and German Catholics more than those of other beliefs, while the Catholics of the Rhineland have the name of being particularly adept at organisation. But in the organisation of cultural associations on a religious basis, their success is not on the whole commensurate with the amount of effort expended. Frequently the members of such organisations maintain their unity not so much out of adherence to the religious principles which are the foundation of their society, as out of a spirit of opposition to other organisations, a desire to count for something or to represent something, or sometimes even the desire to achieve worldly position and prestige. If the political influence of the Church has grown in recent years, it is due not so much to stronger religious convictions on the part of its members as to the fact that the various states have become weaker and now more than ever before need the support of the Church to bolster up their authority undermined by revolutions, bolshevistic threats and social unrest. These techniques of organisation are not to be rejected and it should not be thought that we are finding fault with them; rather the situation which has made their appearance necessary is not altogether a happy one. The colder the iron has been allowed to become, the more it must be hammered before it can be given new form.

Another sign of the lack of popular character by which religion is beset is the fact that the standard-bearers of culture in our age, the men of mature age who know the world, are the ones who are least given to the practice of religion, this being left mainly to women and children and to older men. It would be mere folly to blind our eyes to this fact. It has even been commented upon by so acute an observer as Rathenau in his *Streitschrift vom Glauben*[6] (Polemical discussion of the faith), who says: 'The Church is the communion of saints. Is it not possible that the true communion of the saints is to-day something other than what we know as the

[6] Published by S. Fischer, Berlin 1919, p. 26.

Church, and that for many centuries now the two have been going their separate ways side by side? What guarantee have we that the Church, as we know it, encompasses the living religious spirit of our time?' In the world of to-day, we find all kinds of circles for the advancement of liberal thought and we find Catholics being attracted to such things also. We observe that societies, clubs and brotherhoods under the auspices of the Church have a less vigorous life than do their worldly counterparts. To take just one example, our church choirs generally cannot compare with our male choral groups or glee clubs. We are even forced to conclude that many Catholic laymen, who are by no means hostile to the Church, nevertheless look upon the Church as something taboo.

DIVISIONS WITHIN THE CULTURAL SPHERE

The technical character of modern culture

A greater danger still is the element of decay and corruption introduced into cultural life by its divorce from religion. The christian religion has in its divine origin and guidance a guarantee of freedom from corruption and of preservation and development. Its influence on life may be whittled away by those who profess it, but they can never destroy it. Culture, on the other hand, has no such guarantee, and may decay and wither away. The Sermon on the Mount may lose its influence, but it can never be rejected as a tissue of lies; cultural ideals on the other hand can become distorted and changed. Hence the consequences of this division between culture and life are more fatal for culture. When the bond uniting culture and life goes, then everything suffers as a result. Religion is both a binding influence and at the same time the substantial form of human culture and when it is removed the result must be that the higher and the lower spheres of life disintegrate and fall away from each other. This will lead either to a neglect, culminating in complete disregard, of the higher cultural values or else to a cultivation of these higher values to the exclusion of the lower ones, thus bringing about an esoteric culture, which lacks the solid foundation of a healthy naturalism.

To put the matter more plainly, one will have either, on the one hand, a materialistic attitude to the world and to life or else, on the other, an unreal spiritualism, which exalts the purely spiritual to the point of suppressing and even denying the corporeal factor. Generally, however, it is not the spiritual but the economic element which takes complete precedence and creates a type of person, in regard to whom the word culture is completely out of place. Even piety has become infected by this external, mercenary spirit, which weighs everything from motives of utility and sees religion and religious practices as a means of attaining its ends. The prayer of petition, instead of being for the 'good spirit' as our Saviour directed, is directed towards intentions which have nothing to do with the kingdom of God.[7] True religion becomes mere 'religion to get something out of it', and when the religious practices do not achieve the hoped-for effects and when the earthly intentions which were prayed for are not granted, then faith grows cold. This no doubt explains the universally observed retrogression in the external life of the Church in post-war years; there was a general feeling of disillusion and disappoint-ment among people who felt that religion and faith were of no help to them in their serious economic and political diffi-culties. A religion, which has assumed such a fetish-like character, also suffers the fate of a fetish, namely, to be thrown away as soon as it has outlived its usefulness.

Technical and economic progress are the characteristic features of modern life. Now it is not true, as was generally asserted in the Age of the Enlightenment and as is still alleged by those who look at life and human society from an economic standpoint, that originally the only purpose of life was to bring Nature into subjection so as to make it subservient to man's needs. It can be shown that, even from the very begin-ning, man's labours to bring Nature into subjection were dictated not only by economic and utilitarian considerations but also by less mundane ideas. Science and art, morality and law, even their media of expression, speech and writing, in fact even technical culture and games reveal in their origins a spiritual and even religious character.[8] Even technology, 'the fourth empire' as it is called, possesses a certain spiritual greatness. It is only the mechanisation of life, which subjects the realm of the spirit to technology instead of making technology subject to spiritual needs, which is something evil.

[7] St. Luke 16, 13.
[8] Cf. Alfred Vierkandt, *Der Dualismus im modernen Weltbild*, Berlin 1923, Pan-Verlag Rolf Heise, pp. 13–25.

In an undeveloped culture, however primitive, there is practically no distinction between religion and culture, as has been proved conclusively by recent important discoveries made amongst primitive peoples.[9] A sound and natural process of human development should keep these two elements united: religion and life.

The attitude which judges everything from an economical standpoint leads also to separation and division amongst the various classes and callings in society and in this way also disturbs and destroys the unity of the community. As soon as society loses sight of the ideal of all its constituent classes and callings being united in the pursuit of a common destiny, then it must of necessity fall a prey to that calculating, utilitarian spirit, which replaces rational ends by its own particular aims, concentrates on the means rather than on the end, and winds up by debasing a man's mind and spirit. Thus we find that the civilised man of to-day, in spite of his great intellectual development and his much-vaunted superiority to the external world around him has very little real appreciation of pure religion or of interior sincerity. From this, too, stems the haughty contempt of the modern civilised man for popular forms of religion, such as public processions, and his foolish belief that the value of a person or a society or a people or a cultural epoch can be measured by standards of economic advancement or well-being or by its mean of production.

The most painful and harmful effects of the separation of religion and life are to be seen in the fields of morals and law which are the fields most intimately related with religion. Morality and law derive their chief sanction from religion, and when this sanction goes, then their precepts lose their binding force. That system of morality which has declared itself independent of all religion will soon come to realise its weakness; and ethical culture, which has such confidence in its own autonomy, will soon find itself threatened by a false interpretation of this very autonomy. It is in the domain of marriage, the most basic cell of the whole structure of human society, that the separation of religion and life has wrought the most fearful havoc of all. The contracting of marriage and the conduct of married life have freed themselves almost entirely from any

[9] Cf. Wilhelm Koppers, *Unter Feuerland-Indianern*, Stuttgart 1924, Strecker and Schroder.

Wilhelm Schmidt, *Die Stellung der Pygmäenvolker in der Entwicklungsgeschichte des Menschen*, same publishers, 1910.

religious influence. It is often sad to witness the levity of conduct of bridal couples as they approach the altar of God to enter into a solemn and eternal alliance 'before the Lord God and his holy Church.' Even at a very superficial view of the matter, the increasing number of divorces is a visible symptom of the falling away in regard to matrimony. But we must remember, too, that many more marriages break up internally without any external separation, because there is no spiritual unity between the two parties, and how can this union of souls come about if they are not united in God? The moral conception of marriage, possessed by other ages and peoples, which though crude and carnal to our way of thinking were yet more sound at heart, was, and is, much more desirable than the decadent philosophy of a sophisticated but godless civilisation, which denies the whole sacredness of marriage.

As regards *Law*, its divorce from religion leads to legal positivism, which no longer believes in eternal norms, but makes the State or political advantage the source of law. The idea of the 'partition of the globe' advocated by the juggernaut of imperialistic power with complete disregard for the rights of smaller nations is dubbed by Max Scheler[10] a piece of impious audacity, and he goes on to condemn the incorrigible optimists, who see the position of the Church and the state of the christian conscience of Europe through rose-tinted spectacles in the following terms: 'If all the forces of modern Europe, which are leading us towards a world war, are compatible with the spirit of Christianity or if they are the manifestations of mighty and just strivings, and not deformations which threaten to destroy the existence of European life at its very roots or an intolerable mockery of Christianity, then Christianity has gone bankrupt. If one does not believe that Christianity has gone bankrupt, and has lost its vigour and power, then one must recognise that there has been a radical and widespread apostasy all over Europe, that her representatives have been weak and that her acceptance of and reconciliation with the spirit of anti-Christianity has been unpardonable. There is no way out of this dilemma.' Particularly painful is the realisation that economy has broken loose from the restraining influence of the law of Christ. The introduction of the idea of Might into the

[10] *Vom ewigen im Menschen*, Vol. I: *Religiöse Erneuerung*, Leipzig 1923, Neue Geist Verlag, pp. 308 ff.

world of party politics has led to an element of brute force
and rancour in civil and political life; in fact, in very many
countries in recent years this reached a degree which will
probably never be surpassed.

When even morality and law no longer derive their binding
power from the eternal law of God, then it is obvious that the
utilitarian values are going to break free from any dependence
on the moral values, and hence the way is open for the introduction of a spirit of rationalism which will taint the whole
world. This rationalism is the born enemy of the true life;
it gives rise to the lack of respect for the various mysteries of
life, for the providential order of nature, and for all the various
sources of life, and it also gives rise to a lack of understanding
for that element of symbolism in religion, by which mystery
is best expressed. This explains the modern man's lack of
interest in the solemn and colourful worship of the Church,
in the poetry of religious life and in the popular festivals of
the Church. It also explains the fact so frequently observed
that the children of this world are wiser in their generation
than the children of the light, that is to say, they are more
sure-footed and more diligent in dealing with terrestrial matters
than are pious persons. There is no reason why this should be
so, and it is the fault of men themselves if the strength, which
they can draw upon in spiritual matters, fails them when they
come to tackle the problems of this world.

Rationalism, then, breeds many different types: the intellectual, for whom reason is all-powerful, the man for whom
the human will is lord of all; the man who is a slave to work;
and the man who believes in the law of might alone. It produces
the worldly man, who uses his superior intelligence to deceive
the simple people around him; the heartless man, who by
reason of his better acquaintance with the written laws can
break the laws of nature, especially the law of love, with
impunity; the soulless man, who has lost the faculty of appreci-
ating or savouring the things of the spirit; and the pharisaical
type, who by confounding external observance with inner
piety perverts the true worship of God, which consists, according to the words of Holy Scripture, in the following: '. . . to give
aid to orphans and widows in their tribulation, and to keep
oneself unspotted from this world.'[11]

[11] James 1, 27.

The dualism in modern cultural life

The cultural life of our age has lost all unity. In spite of the numerous international alliances of the present day, there is no real unity amongst peoples nor amongst the members of any one people, nor is there anywhere to be found a unified harmonious popular culture. And how can there be a harmonious popular culture, when neither unity nor harmony reigns within the individual himself? The pursuit of and the possession of a great deal of knowledge is not synonymous with culture: a mere external conjunction of inorganic parts does not form an organic whole; likewise, an agglomeration of talent and of supplies of knowledge, which do not become a unified whole within the whole man, does not deserve the name of culture. There is no use in laying the blame on mechanisation and technical development as such, since these are the products of an inevitable process of development. With the increase in the world's population it becomes harder to maintain the production of the necessities of life and the struggle for existence becomes harder, and so the human intellect must devise ways and means to preserve the life of the world. It is not therefore this levelling process, which subjects everything to technique and method, that is wrong in itself, but rather the fact that it tends to kill the soul of life. It is hardly possible to enumerate all the disorders which follow upon this process; there is conflict between science and religion, between philosophy and science, and again between science and life, between the State and the Nation, between civil and political life, between religion and Eros and between ethics and Eros, and innumerable other such conflicts.

There is conflict between the christian peoples. Races, nations and states are virtually at war with one another. European Christendom is in a sad state when it pursues this warfare with unchristian, nay even diabolical, weapons and that it does not hesitate to call to its aid savage and pagan peoples. And moreover, this warfare is aimed at annihilation of the enemy. Nationalism has proved superior to the spirit of religion; the ties of blood and of culture have prevailed over the ties of grace and the christian faith, and even religion has become the servant of nationalism. The idea of the catholic unity of the nations seems to be lost sight of.

The conflict amongst the nations has, as a corollary, conflict amongst the members of each people; and this in turn leads to a state of conflict between individual souls. The idea of the people as an organic unity no longer exists; in fact, the word 'folk', when attached to other words, has now come to have reference solely to the lower classes of society, which shows that the old concept of the folk as a united people has given way to a division into an upper class, which calls itself the cultured class, and lower class, which has no share in the benefits of culture. It has been observed that the onset of war often makes a people conscious of their unity, but it is not a true or permanent unity, and dissolves as soon as the war or the threat of war recedes. All the ordinances of society, the family, the parish, the province, exist by the will of God and even when incorporated by the State retain their own individual rights. They cannot be set aside by the might of the State, nor can they be obliged to sacrifice anything of their particular lives, except in so far as the well-being of the State absolutely necessitates it. The State, however, which does not recognise God, tends to ignore the rights of these institutions sanctioned by God and nature, and to bring everything under its own control, because it believes and can believe only in Might and in the success of Might. We find an unhealthy individualism all along the line: an exaggerated emphasis on personality, sentiment, goodwill as against objective goodness, the means of knowledge as opposed to the truth, the formal element in art, science and oratory, as against the material factor, an excessive cult of personal prestige and of intellectual distinction, a hankering after originality—these are phenomena, which have always been natural to man to some extent, but which in our day have come to the fore to an unprecedented degree.

Within the nations and the states the division into political parties prevails and seems likely to assume even greater proportions in the future. And again within these very same parties, even the parties which profess themselves christian in outlook and as having the welfare of the whole people in mind, there are further divisions caused by the particular interests of the various groups and social classes or by the economic circumstances of the members. In the German parliament, more than elsewhere on the Continent, we see this picture of division and subdivision. It is not the outstanding candidate, the man with sound political acumen and breadth of vision, who is voted in but rather the representative of a particular group, whose first duty and care it will be to further the interests of this group. In the councils of the political parties, as in the councils of the nations, it is the idea of Might which holds sway and not that of truth and justice, let alone love; and this holds both for victors and vanquished. In trying to pin the guilt for past events on each other, they fail to realise that Europe and the whole world has a share in that guilt. It is a question, then, of fighting for mastery and self-justification rather than for the establishment of truth and justice. However, so long as all parties fail to realise that the guilt of past calamities must be shared by all, there can be no reform of the parties or of their political and moral principles.

The classes are divided. One sometimes gets the impression that it is not the same people who comprise the different classes. Instead of a spirit of honest rivalry, the driving forces in social life are envy, mistrust, the lust for power. There is a conflict between the classes, which reaches the pitch of actual hate. Little effort is made towards mutual understanding each class judges the other in the light of its own prejudices. Oppression and exploitation on the one hand are answered by resistance and strikes on the other; and the confidence and mutual trust, which should exist between men and Christians, give place to mistrust and motives of self-interest. It is the same capitalistic spirit which motivates the conduct of both haves and have-nots, bourgeoisie and proletariat.

There is even a struggle between the sexes, a struggle unknown in former times. If this conflict between the sexes were nothing more than the outcome of a cultural movement, which it is in part, it would be highly desirable as the manifestation of a spirit of emulation and a desire on the part of woman to raise herself from a condition of inferiority. The feminist movement is, in fact, a cultural movement, in which woman is awakening to an awareness of her own personality and her value and significance for society. From the economic point of view, its origin may be seen in the difficult economic conditions which create an obstacle to marriage and prevent woman from pursuing her proper vocation; from the cultural viewpoint it has its origins in the increasing soullessness of life in general, and of family life in particular and in fact that man, and even woman herself, has lost sight of the christian and human dignity of woman. Biologically, it results from a failure to recognise the polarity between the two sexes. When the essential difference between man and woman is ignored, it may seem to bring the sexes closer together whereas in reality it only leads to an estrangement between them, since one or the other, if not both, renounces the characteristics proper to it thus destroying that relation of tension, which alone makes true unity possible.

Woman suffers more than man from the increasing material-isation of life and from the triumph of technology. From the subjective point of view, man suffers less from it, because it is he who has created this specifically masculine culture and also because it is his vocation to be always striving for domin-ance over nature, whereas the woman's vocation, as giver and preserver of life, is the preservation of her own physical and moral health in accordance with the sacred laws of nature. It is not the nature of woman to excel in intellect or in the capacity for hard physical work; in fact, the woman, who devotes herself to the academic life, in adapting herself to a culture which is largely masculine in origin, loses something of her womanhood and binds herself to an undertaking which wastes her functional energies. But culture ought not to be a masculine thing nor a feminine thing; it ought to be simply human and christian, since in Christianity there is 'neither male nor female.'[12]

The creation of such a human and christian culture is a task which presents itself to women as well as to men; without the cooperation of woman, culture is apt to fall short of true human nobility and take on a note of imperious harshness, while without the cooperation of man culture would receive a certain effeminate character. When the mind takes precedence of the soul and intelligence is preferred to love, when a healthy attitude of mind gives place to an unhealthy spirit of calculation and self-interest, then it is obvious that woman is going to be considered as something inferior and is going to suffer in her personal dignity; and on the other hand, when woman loses contact with the sources of life, religion and nature, then she falls into a state of degeneration and the culture of a people or a family or a society is doomed to decline.

There is a conflict between science and life. It is only in accordance with the inner workings of science that it must keep at a certain distance from its subject; before it puts its subject under the looking-glass, it must freeze it or 'kill' it, so to speak. The progress of science demands an ever-greater degree of specialisation, and this, by keeping the eye fixed on smaller segments of life, can easily lose contact with living reality. But the gap between science and life has become wider than the nature of science would demand. For science is a part

[12] Galatians 3, 28.

of life, one of the most noble and beautiful manifestations of
the intellectual life, and there is no reason why it should be
bound hand and foot and placed at the service of technology.

Science is also wisdom; the goal of all philosophy is 'sophia';
science can maintain an attitude of reference before life and
the mysteries of life, and should not presume to lift the veil
from those things, which are beyond its scope. It is free to
explore all the avenues of reality, always realising however,
that the highest form of knowledge in this life is the knowledge
of faith. Many examples exist to prove that science and philosophy have owed some of their strongest stimuli to the religious
interest taken by a person or an age or a society in some
profane object of knowledge; the history of religion and the
science of comparative religion owe their origin and development to Christianity's claim to be the one true religion, while
the science of comparative anthropology and the theories of
evolution were the outcome of interest in the biblical account
of the creation of man and the science of textual criticism
owes its rise to the dogma of Inspiration. In every intellectual
investigation there is a latent *religious point of view*, whether
it be favourable or hostile. And even in times or amongst men
who have been hostile to religion or the Church—and let us
remember that this hostility itself is symptomatic of interest—
the desire to undermine the religious position and to prove it
false has given added attraction to research in the profane
sciences. In the extreme phase of the separation of religion and
life, when the two spheres have lost contact completely,
scientific investigation can take on a note of asceticism,
occupying itself heroically with a subject which has no attraction for it and which it tackles to achieve some purpose and has
no relation to life.

This negative attitude of science to life does not believe in
the main stream of science and philosophy in which succeeding
generations add their mite to the storehouse of knowledge
filled by their predecessors; rather does it believe in men of
genius, who are outside this main stream of development, but
who nevertheless are the men who influence and determine
the form of life. It is sufficient to mention the names of
Keyserling, Steiner and Kierkegaard. Just as the life of big
cities tends to isolate the citizens from nature, in the same
way science removes the intellectual life from nature; the one
leads men away from nature and from the natural institutions
of family and society, from nature, which has always been the

fountainhead of spiritual and religious vigour. The other breaks the bonds which link man to the present world and the world hereafter, except, of course, where science is aware of the need to maintain contact with life. Such being the case, it is no longer a source of wonder, that those who are engaged in scientific investigation fall away more easily from religion and church, than the uneducated, whose naturally christian spirit preserves them from the danger of such perversion. 'How often', says Hermann Platz,[13] 'has a self-conscious attitude of infallibility been just the mask to conceal the marks of suffering in the soul, to conceal the discontent caused by being forced to run aground in the stagnant pools of specialisation and the yearning to burst forth into the original freshness of life's turbulent waters.'

It was the consciousness of this gulf between science and life which led academic circles some years ago to cry out for the establishment of a 'humanistic faculty', whose task it would be to bring the sciences into unity with each other and with life.[14] Even Schopenhauer mocks the alienation of science from life and draws a distinction between scholars and thinkers, between those who have read books and those who have read in the book of life; and a famous German disciple of Rembrandt[15] commented that the number of people in Germany wearing spectacles to see material objects was only equal to the number of those who were short-sighted in regard to the things of the spirit. Even the language, which is its medium of expression, with its wholly unjustifiable ambiguity, shows how far the science of our times is removed from life. However, in this regard also, there are signs that a healthy reaction is beginning to set in: in the movement away from subjectivism; the conscious attempt to find a comprehensive system of metaphysics; the tendency amongst modern thinkers to think in terms of a philosophy of life; and the emphasis placed by phenomenology on the value of the objective, we can perceive, in spite of some obscurities, signs of an effort to find a new approach to life,

The German is more deeply affected by all these divisions than the people of other nations. They even, according to

[13] *Grossstadt und Menschentum*, Munich 1924, Kösel and Pustet, p. 12.

[14] *Zeitschrift für Hochschulpädagogik XIII*, Leipzig 1922, K. F. Köhler, pp. 3 ff.

[15] *Rembrandt als Erzieher*, von einem Deutschen, Leipzig 1922, C. L. Hirschfeldt, p. 45.

Max Scheler,[16] leave their imprint on the external appearance of the German, so that 'all foreigners, who have compared notes on this point, are agreed that the external appearance of the German betrays his class and profession at once, whether he is officer, professor, scholar, merchant or whatever else he may be.' The rapid development of the German Empire, in the years after its victorious wars, from an agricultural state into a great industrial power meant that, with the economic advance there went hand in hand a great progress in technology and that lacking the counterweight of a sufficiently strong religion, the German soul was drawn into the maelstrom and became a slave to this technology. And the more a church tends to influence the life of a man in other respects, the more does this gulf between religion and life make itself felt; hence its effects are more marked in the case of the Catholics, for whom his church plays a very important role, than in the adherents of other beliefs.

This explains why the unfortunate campaign of Liberalism against the Catholic Church could presume to term itself a 'Kulturkampf', or cultural war. For a long time, German Catholics had to suffer the reproach of inferiority in silence, without being able to do anything effective to rid themselves of it; but in the last two decades the Catholics have become more aware of their duty to cooperate in facing the literary, philosophical and theological problems of the present day and, by pulling their weight in the struggle to solve these problems, they have silenced this reproach. Nevertheless, the basic outlines of the relation between religion and life have remained essentially the same. It only remains to be hoped that, when the present technological system breaks down and reveals itself unable to answer all the problems of life, it will be the occasion for the fundamentally religious character of the German to look within itself and to bring itself once more into alignment with the past. At least it is to be hoped that the more sensitive and thoughtful souls will do so.

The more foresighted thinkers of our times have raised their voices in warning and have urged the abolition of this dualism of religion and life. F. W. Foerster in the periodical 'Die Menschheit'[17] (Humanity) says: 'We have now reached a moment of crisis for Western civilisation: either Christian

[16] *Christentum und Gesellschaft*, first half-vol.: *Konfessionen*, Leipzig 1924, Der Neue Geist Verlag, p. 18.
[17] Vol. 10, 1923, No. 23 (9 June), p. 115.

culture will triumph over our politico-moral paganism, or else the barbarism of our so-called civilisation will drive out Christian culture; the latter will then be obliged to take refuge amongst the peoples of the Orient, from whence it originally came.' He goes on to recall how Rabindranath Tagore had asserted at a lecture in Tokyo some time previously, that the West was in the throes of a decline owing to a disastrous division between religion and life. This division was basically the expression of a deep lack of real belief in the things of the spirit and a manifestation of a deadly materialism, which had infected large sections of society whose religious traditions and forms were sterile and devoid of any real vitality or power. He saw this materialism as a deadly blight withering their spiritual potential and threatening the whole spiritual future of the West. He said that it rested with the coming generations whether the present unhappy situation would deteriorate to such a degree as to bring about the downfall of the West or whether the last moment, would witness the triumph of a spiritual regeneration.

It does our Western Christian culture no credit that the spiritual leaders of the Orient are beginning to openly extol their own culture as superior to ours. Thus Mahatma Gandhi, the great religious and political leader of the Indian people, writes: 'The last war has revealed the satanic nature of the civilisation which dominates Europe to-day. In the name of justice all the laws of public morality have been violated by the victors. No lie was too base to be availed of. And the reason for all these crimes is a gross materialism. Europe is no longer Christian; her God is Mammon.'[18] And the following appraisal of christian culture comes from an article published by a Moslem in Count Keyserling's 'Schule der Weisheit' (The School of Wisdom):[19] 'The Europeans are civilised, but in their hearts they have little culture! They have railways, electric light, telegraph and telephone, but culturally they are very backward. Avarice and self-interest, these are the gods that they adore.' It is beneficial for us to listen to such judgements, especially because they come from strangers and rivals, since we ourselves are too sunk in our own vices and in our spiritual poverty to be able to see our position accurately.

This cry of 'the decline of the West' continues to ring in our

[18] Romain Rolland, *Mahatma Gandhi*, Erlenbach-Zürich 1922, Rotapfel Verlag, p. 35 ff.
[19] *Der Leuchter* V (1924), p. 124.

ears and gives us no rest. We realise instinctively that if we do not succeed in finding the path of return to a true Christianity and thereby to our true and better selves this will be our actual fate. If the West is to decline, it will not be in accordance with any biological law, which decrees that no civilisation can outlive a certain age and that just as it rose, so, too, must it inevitably fall; rather will it decline because it misused its freedom in introducing a separation or gulf between religion and life. Precisely how the unity of religion and life is to be effected no one can say; but much would have been achieved if we could be brought to realise that it no longer exists and that it must be restored. The difficulty lies in the fact that our Nature is no longer Nature but has taken on a note of the unnatural, and that our Christianity is no longer truly christian but has taken on a note of pharisaic sham, mixed with superstition and idolatry. Only a gradual process of renovation can restore a healthy state of tension between religion and life. The unfortunate thing about this process is that each one must recover its true self before they can enter into a proper relationship with each other, that each one must first have regained its own health before it can help to heal the other. Culture cannot become true culture until it has become christian, and Christianity cannot be truly christian unless it builds on the foundation of healthy nature and assimilates it into itself.

There is a paradox here, but there is something mysteriously paradoxical in the growth of all things, the same paradox which is found in life itself. For to live is 'to move oneself', but how can anything move itself, since we know that 'everything, which moves, is moved by something else'? We have the same paradox in the life of the spirit, that the spirit always strives for the evolution of its own being; so also do science and philosophy, which, though they have their own being, can never fully realise the perfection of this being. Thus a true unity of religion and life is not something which can be simply achieved: it is something which must evolve, and this organic evolution is a vital process. All that man and humanity can do is to create the conditions favourable to this process of evolution by which the lost unity is to be re-established, to prepare the ground and remove any weeds which would prevent the seed of new life from reaching the light. Religion and life are of their very natures designed for a most intimate and close relationship with each other, and no matter what distortions or deformations appear in them, both are still sound at root and are capable of restoration to perfect vigour and health. This restoration will all the sooner come to pass, the more man retains his reverence for the mysteries of life. He can learn much about this reverence from the Asiatic spirit, which, however little its regard for our intellectuality, has often greater sensitivity vis-a-vis the problems of life.

Our culture, cut adrift from religion, Christianity and Church, feels deeply the emptiness and isolation of its position and longs for the re-establishment of a union between religion and life, Christianity and humanity, Church and world. But it will find great difficulty in admitting its errors; and since an examination of religion shows certain signs of decadence and failure, as it must inevitably do, culture seizes eagerly upon these regrettable features in order to take refuge behind them and to reject the Church altogether. There is a strange wavering between a consciousness of guilt and an obstinate hardheartedness, between a longing to be reconciled and a reluctance to make a humble admission of guilt. The two sides hesitate and waver and would like to come closer to each other; but religion and life, the Church and the culture of the world have lived too long apart to be immediately reunited and reconciled. However, some day it will come about, as it must come about, for neither one can live without the other and each feels itself alone and impoverished. It is like two men, who lived and played together as children and who later have gone different ways ; when they meet again after many years, they do not know whether they should avoid or greet each other, but then happy memories of those carefree childhood days and of the joys they shared awake in their souls, and they greet each other and soon recover their former mutual sympathy and understanding. It may be, however, that in the case of religion and life, the time is not yet ripe for mutual understanding to be re-established. It may be that our European culture has to become yet more conscious of its misery before it can find the humility to decide on return and reform.

However, there are indications that the end of the road is near; that the paths of religion and life are coming closer together and that both feel a reunion to be an urgent necessity. Certain currents of thought amongst modern youth, literary phenomena, religious circles and associations, and societies for the advancement of christian culture are all heralds of a new departure, which give grounds for feeling hope and enthusiasm; nevertheless, the fall was so great and the disillusionment so intense that it would be presumptuous to hope for a spiritual rebirth of Europe in our generation. This incipient process of spiritual rebirth, 'if it is to be something more than a mere flickering up of goodwill or good intentions, must nourish itself on the shame and sorrow of what has so recently happened amongst Christians themselves; we refer to the world war.'[20]

It is gratifying to see a widespread return to Metaphysics, but we must remember that it was not the Catholic, but the non-Catholic philosophers, who took the initiative in a return to unity in this domain of philosophy. It was only after they led the break away from subjectivism, which was at once foreign to life and hostile to faith, and re-discovered the heritage of Scholasticism, that our Catholic philosophers have begun to recognise this heirloom, which the Church had never parted with and to rejoice in the possession of it and to look, presumptuously perhaps, to the dawn of a new era of Catholic culture. In the light of these considerations, who can refrain from thinking of the Pauline parable of the olive tree and the branches broken off and grafted on?[21]

[20] Karl Borromäus Heinrich, *Das Gesicht des deutschen Katholizismus, gesehen von einem Laien,* Munich 1924, Franz Pfeiffer and Co., p. 9.
[21] Romans 11, 15–36.

4
Our duty
to unify religion and life

Human nature is designed for unity. But this unity is not a
gratuitous gift: it is something which must be striven for.
It is only in the infancy both of man and of the human race
that we find this unity in the form of a natural and unconscious
equilibrium. Thus, for instance, the Middle Ages is the infancy
of christian culture and has all the charm of childhood. But
the child tends towards manhood, and we cannot turn back
the clock and return to childhood. The ingenuous and happy
unity between religion and life in primitive times is gone,
never to return. History cannot go backwards, anymore than
rivers reverse their course and return to the mountains from
which they have come. We may find here and there a remote
place still untouched by civilisation, in which the happy state
of cultural infancy still persists, and we may with the poet
sing the idyllic life of those who inhabit these places who
have not yet felt the breath of freedom but live out their lives
in cheerful obedience to the laws of nature. But we must
reckon with reality; we do not wish to remain children, and it
is undesirable and impossible to recall the patriarchal conditions of primitive times. We have been carried too far by
our cultural impulses for that; we have become too attached
to culture and to cultural values. We can, will, and ought to
become children again only in the sense that we adopt a
position of conscious unity or better still, that we strive to
achieve a constant balance between the forces which oppose
each other in a relation of tension, with a resultant ennobling
of our whole being. Thus we would reconcile the warring

poles of our nature and still the longing of our nature for active repose.

We must transform the potential energy of this new state of tension into kinetic energy, which can be utilised to contribute to the advancement of humanity and to the setting up of the kingdom of God. And vigilant spirits will be able to find positive attitudes to life, and ways and means of loving and advancing culture without doing violence to conscience nor incurring the danger of degeneracy and falling into unculture. We must now examine the means which present themselves for this purpose and see which of them are most adapted to our needs.

HOW UNION MAY BE ACHIEVED

For the sake of clarity, we will first state that by religion we understand the subordination of man to God and by life we mean the cultivation of temporal values. We are taking life, therefore, in the restricted sense of cultural life, and we restrict cultural values, in turn, to purely terrestrial values. The subject of religion is the whole man, and the subject of culture or of life is likewise man, as such. Both religion and life, therefore, lay claim to the whole man. Both belong to man's essential nature: man is naturally as religious as he is cultural; he has a need of culture and a duty towards it.

Our problem is not to remove the tension between religion and life, since this tension is a law of life. In fact, this state of tension can never be reduced to a condition of equilibrium, because it is in the nature of the two forces to produce work continuously by their interaction in the same subject, namely, man, and because their spheres of operation are not contiguous but are interwoven in each other. These spheres have reference to God, who in respect of the world is at once immanant and transcendent, and to the world, which has to be made divine. Thus we see how the destruction of equilibrium is continually giving rise to new tensions, which in turn try to balance each other in order to regain equilibrium. This equilibrium, then, is the ideal which is striven for, but it cannot be realised in the present life, because it is the active repose of eternity. This longing for repose, which is inherent in man, the desire to re-establish the equilibrium which has been disturbed by the operation of forces at opposing poles, impels the two forces to transform their potential energy into kinetic energy and thus to release in an ever-increasing measure their reservoirs of latent power. It is thus that this urge for repose becomes the source of continuous and unlimited progress.

The possible forms of approach to, or alienation from God and the world may be reduced to four: separation from the world in order to approach more closely to God, separation from God in order to give oneself to the world, approach to God by way of the world, and approach to the world by way of God. These give us four typical attitudes to religion and life: the service of God, the service of the world, service of God by serving the world and the service of the world by serving God. These four attitudes, in turn, are the basis of four different types of life: the life which deserts God for the culture of the world, the life which serves God and despises the world, the life which serves God while pursuing the culture of the world, and the life which occupies itself with the things of the world and therein serves God. In the first case, life is alien and hostile to religion, in the second, religion maintains itself aloof from and hostile to life, in the third, religion is well-disposed to life and in the fourth, life is well-disposed to religion.

The first type is that of pure humanism: a pagan cult of noble humanity, in so far as humanity without religion can be noble. When we describe it as pagan, we are not thinking of idolatrous paganism, although indeed the cult of pure humanity is in itself a form of idolatry since, from the religious point of view, any over-estimation of terrestrial values with a disparagement of spiritual values may with reason be termed a 'refinement of idolatry'. In its most elevated form this type of culture pledges itself to the cultivation of the natural terrestrial values in the order of their importance, with a complete disregard for the supernatural values.

The second type is that of pure mysticism, which knows and recognises only God and despises all else as evil or of no consequence. This has its prototype in the ancient religions of India and in Manichaeism which regards the world as something negative or as an apostasy from the Absolute or as the work of an evil primary principle, in short, as something essentially evil. This type can be easily reduced to the first type: in the one it is God, in the other the world, which becomes an illusion or a fiction; in the one the world is deified and worshipped, in the other the whole world is absorbed in God. For both types there is no difference between God and the world.

The third type is that of mystic union with God which has nevertheless a humanistic character; it goes through and beyond this world to achieve a state of union with the Godhead. It is well-disposed to the world and its culture, nevertheless it views it as a transitory state which must be overcome.

The fourth type is a humanism with a mystical character; it gives itself with conviction and entire confidence to the world and to its ends, to a world, however, which comes from God and which is intimately united with him, in whose image it is made, and to the demands of worldly culture which it sees as imposed by God. It is, therefore, a cooperation in the work of divinising the world and man.

These types which we have outlined are naturally never found in all their purity; what we actually find is countless combinations of the main types, in which now one, now another tendency predominates. These combinations give rise to new tensions between the various types, which tensions engender new teleological currents in the onward march of the world and thereby introduce a new element of beauty into the life of men and of the world.

Already at this point we can state that the first two types outlined afford no real solution to the problems of religion and life. They destroy the tension between religion and life, between God and the world, and they reduce to a mere fiction any opposition of polarity, since there are no longer any opposing forces: either God or the world is made absolute, either religion or life. Only the third and fourth types, then, can be considered as acceptable solutions. Both adopt an affirmative attitude to God and the world, to religion and life, to Christianity and culture, to supernatural sanctity and to noble humanity; the difference between them is that they have a different way of constructing the parallelogram of forces, as it is called. Likewise they have a different notion of man's duty vis-à-vis the world; the one aims to overcome the world, the other to help in perfecting it and making it divine.

When they consider this world into which they have been born, men sometimes feel with a sense of disillusionment that although it is one of God's works, it still is not God, and they conceive the desire to have as little contact as possible with the world but to devote all their energies to the service of God. But the same consideration may cause other men to throw all their energies into the task of making this imperfect world approach as closely as possible to the image of the Creator.

The first line of thought is made the pretext for discarding the purely natural order as much as possible and clinging to God alone, while the second leads to a desire for collaboration in shaping the new world in the divine image. Those who hold the latter position may be said to rejoice in the world: not, however, in the world as it is *de facto*, but rather in the world as it is to become by the natural efforts of man. Now, I have spoken of the third type as being well-disposed to the world, but this type is often termed ill-disposed to the world or thought to be avoiding the world, as opposed to those who take an affirmative attitude to the world; in fact, the representatives of this type generally speak of the world as something which they have abandoned and as the antithesis of the kind of life which they have chosen for their own. This apparent contradiction is due, however, to an ambiguity in the meaning which is attached to the word 'world'. By it we can understand the 'wicked' world which has turned its back on God and which it is the moral duty of any religious man to shun. Or we can understand it to mean the physical world as God's Creation and the manifestation of his glory, the setting of the life and miracles of his divine Son, and the location of man and of human society; in this sense, it is impossible for us to abandon it, rather are we morally bound to remain in it, for man belongs to Creation and is a member of human society as well as of the kingdom of God, and so he must take part in all those institutions which are of the divine will. But even in this notion of the world, the whole position of each of the two types cannot be wrapped up neatly under the labels 'well-disposed or attached to the world' and 'hostile to the world', for the latter cannot and must not and does not wish to flee the world entirely, as taken in this sense, and the former cannot and must not and does not wish to be absorbed completely in the service of the world. So there is not a question of two extremes, but rather of two positions which differ only in degree; a more and a less. For the one must occupy himself with the things of the world, at least in the measure that they impinge on his own being, and he also avails of the world in so far as it serves to bring him closer to God; the other cannot serve the world without also serving God as well, because the world is God's world after all. In view of this, it would perhaps be more fitting for us to call the former of these two religious types the mystic type, and the other the activistic type.

INADEQUATE SOLUTIONS TO THE PROBLEM

The first two types, whatever their general importance as philosophic conceptions of the world, need not detain us here very long, since they do not give any satisfactory answer to the problem of the relationship between religion and life. For the one God is everything, while for the other the world is everything; and in a very broad sense they both contain a religious element, in so far as every man devotes himself to the service of some good, which for him is the Supreme Good. 'Our finite consciousness', says Max Scheler,[1] 'is not free to believe in anything. Every man, who examines himself and others closely, will find that there is always some good or principle with which he identifies himself so closely that his relation to it may be summed up in the words: "Without you, in which I believe, I can not be, I do not want to be, I must not be. We two, you and I, O Good, we stand and fall together".' This good varies, of course, for different individuals, peoples, classes and so on; in fact, it is of infinite variety. For those who worship Mammon it is gold, for those who idolise the State it is the State, for those whose highest good is the nation it is the nation; for the child it may be its doll. But man must believe either in God or in some such idol. There is no other alternative!' In neither case can there be any question of a real state of tension between religion and life. If God is the only reality and all else is only an illusion, then life itself is only an illusion. But if the world is the only perfect reality and if God is only a fiction of the intellect, then religion also is only a fiction. In neither case can true religion or life flourish; true life cannot, since only the Absolute, be it God or the world, exists and gives life to man; and true religion cannot, since religion demands a real relation, a subordination of man to God, not to a God who is conceived as a mere abstraction but to a God who has a real personal existence, transcendent and at the same time immanent to the world.

The religious position of the world-hater and despiser is simply an exaggeration of the oriental attitude. The Oriental is tempted to doubt the infallibility of the senses which only

[1] *Vom Ewigen im Menschen* I, 197 f.

bring the illusion of an existing world before his eyes, and of the intellect which only brings contradictions to light. His deep instinctive sense of the problem of phenomena and of the unfathomable enigma of being do not permit an unquestioning faith in the values of this world.[2] He accepts the dualism between appearance and reality with fatal resignation and bows reverently before the mystery of being: 'His fear is elevated into worship, his resignation has become a religion.'[3] On the other hand, the frame of mind which turns its back on God and clings to the world is simply the European mode of thought and life carried to an extreme. Over a period of thousands of years, the struggle with nature in the northern regions of the earth has given man a deep rooted interest in the world and in the means of bringing it under his control and domination, and it has endowed the European man with a remarkable bodily and spiritual aptitude for work. The mode of life, which is based on aversion and hostility to the world, finds its expression in the pantheistic conception of the world and of life and also in an elevated mysticism; while the mode of life which clings to the world and ignores God, finds its expression as a philosophic conception of the universe in Monism and as an attitude to the problem of existence in humanism. It is no accident, but for reasons which follow logically from the basic principles which govern them, that these two approaches to the world and to life often become so alike as to be indistinguishable. Sometimes the universe or some part of it is made by some religious theory to take on a divine character, and thus an atheistic Monism becomes religious Pantheism; and sometimes, the Godhead is conceived as the whole universe, and then religious Pantheism has become a materialistic Monism. Then again, humanism, in the sense of the fullest possible development of man's purely human faculties, is sometimes made into a religion, while at other times true religion is seen in the exaltation of human nature and personality.

The first type of the person, who clings to God and shuns the world is found also, though not in all its purity, amongst most ancient Asiatic peoples, especially the Brahmins and Buddhists, who in the various forms of theosophy and anthroposophy and in neo-Buddhism celebrate a kind of ressur-

[2] Wilhelm Worringer, *Formprobleme der Gothik* Munich 1922, R. Piper and Co., p. 24.

[3] loc. cit., p. 25.

rection or re-incarnation not at all dissimilar to that envisaged by very mystically-minded Christians. To this class also belongs the elevated mysticism which is common to all ages, in which God and the world, body and soul, the here and the hereafter are seen not as in an opposition of polarity but in open contradiction. The world is eliminated altogether, or its existence is denied. Or else it is seen as something essentially evil, hostile to God, the product of an evil principle, as with the Manichaeans. Life is traduced, the body is ignored, culture is despised and the world hated. The whole aim of life is the absorption into a nirvana, which, though not perhaps absolute nothingness, is nevertheless a condition of impersonal existence.

It is clear that this view makes any kind of union between religion and life absolutely impossible. Life is not considered as a value at all, and personal existence is seen as the root of all suffering in the world. This type seeks to discard the human factor and would even like to eliminate it altogether. Buddhist asceticism, for instance, has designed a formal technique, which aims at the gradual weaning away of oneself from existence,[4] and which avails of such exercises as the prolonged contemplation of a decomposed corpse or of a leering skull wreathed in snakes. It goes without saying that such a way is not for us, if only because of our conception of God as a God, whose goodness and truth are incompatible with such a deceitful and evil world. It is chiefly in Monism, as the more enlightened formulation of a naive Pantheism, that the notion of God is so adulterated as to make him unknowable. But one would need to have closed one's eyes completely to the tragedy of human life and of the world's woes to confuse human nature or the world with God. Any illusion of religion that there may be in this philosophy of the world recedes when some partial good within the universe is constituted as the highest good, and the more limited this good is, the more does the philosophy appear unadulterated mockery of religion. The very dignity of human nature itself makes this view untenable. For man is not a pure spirit, the body is not essentially opposed to the soul, and the union between the two is not a mere passing one nor the product of a mere accident nor a punishment for some fault committed; rather do body and soul form an internal, natural and substantial unity, and the body, too, is a work of the Creator, an image both of God and of the human

---

[4] Cf. Friedrich Heiler, *Die buddhistische Versenkung*, an essay in religious history, Munich 1922, Ernst Reinhardt, p. 19 f.

spirit, the companion of the soul, called with it to share in its glory.

The second type, that of the man who clings to the world and turns his back on God, is found mainly in the domain of humanism. Here it is not the world as a whole that occupies the centre of the stage, but rather man; the cultivation of pure humanity is its watchword. It is the form of life which devotes itself to cultivating the natural nobility of man. By contrast with Christianity one can also describe it as a form of neo-paganism, in which life and culture are everything. And bearing out what we have said about the tendency of life, when released from the control of religion, to split up into further divisions, we find the varied goods of this world being made into absolute values and being regarded as the central meaning of life, science or learning, a morality independent of religion, art, the development of personality, the progress of mankind; nation, State, riches, work, love or pleasure. In its most perfect form, of course, humanism does not isolate any of these values but combines them all and cultivates them in the order of their importance. The type of noble humanity could be the Greek of classical times, if he were such a man as the Renaissance loved to portray him, or as he was visualised by Winckelmann or even more so by Goethe, who admired him for his artistic spirit, his oneness with nature and his joy in life, and even went further by holding him up as a model in everything relating to the conduct of life.[5] From the time of the Enlightenment such people as Wilhelm von Humboldt might be chosen as specimens of noble humanity, even though in their case also a deeper scrutiny would show that they also made notable concessions to human frailty.[6] This type could take as its motto the phrase of Goethe's Faust: 'He who has science and art has also religion; and let he who has neither of these have religion.' Whatever this phrase may mean in the context of the Faust drama, Goethe himself later paraphrased it by asserting that science and art and culture in general can and should replace religion, and that culture represents a higher stage in the development of religion.

This type of pagan cultivation of noble humanity is the most treacherous and dangerous enemy of Christianity at the present time; and its danger lies in the fact that outwardly it so

[5] Cf. Wilhelm Lütgert, *Die Religion des deutschen Idealismus und ihr Ende*, I, 115 ff.

[6] loc. cit., pp. 122–124.

resembles the christian mode of life which embraces the world as its path to God, that although there is a world of difference between them, it is not such as to reveal itself to the superficial beholder. To the European, whose attitude was nurtured by the Enlightenment, whose mind and senses are so subtle and adept when there is question of grasping and subjugating natural phenomena, this style is more dangerous and seductive than it is for the man of simple faith who is close to nature, or for the Oriental or Mediterranean man, whose less complex civilisation permits him to retain a better instinctive power of reaction. This type has become more and more widespread, until it is now the most dangerous rival which Christianity has to fear in Europe or in America. This shows, then, that the opposition of the different conceptions of the world and of life comes to a head with the opposition of the purest forms of religion and irreligion in man. For instance, Nietzsche's Superman, who dethroned and killed God and set himself up in his place, did, it is true, carry godless culture to its ultimate conclusion; nevertheless, he was immediately followed, re-actionwise, by a vivid awareness of the terrible desolation and emptiness experienced by the disinherited soul. Newman reduces all the systems of conceiving the world to an ultimate opposition between atheism and Catholicism.

We only wish to stress here that these two forms of regarding religion and life make any kind of union impossible, since the two forces do not stand on the same level. The one is on the level of reality, the other on the level of intellectual fiction; hence the contact between them, which is necessary for a relation of tension, does not exist. We may observe in passing that these forms of thought distort completely the essence of religion as a true relation between really existing human nature and a real personal God, something inherent in man's very nature. Without religion there can be no such things as noble humanity. Reality has no life or existence in itself, if it tries to stand without God or if it excludes God, and even less if it defies God; it tends to fall into annihilation, and the only thing which can keep it out of the abyss of nothingness and lift it into existence is the stream of power radiating from the God-head. As Scheler puts it so strikingly, 'That is how the world appears, when left to its own devices: death becomes a void, the capacity for work becomes a capacity for destruction, life becomes death, and the spirit is engulfed in the maelstrom of life, dragged down by the impulses of instinct and the fires of passion. This fallen world is dominated by an irresistible decline from higher values to lower values, the source of ever-growing miseries and ever stronger temptations to evil for spiritual natures.[7] Man, as a free being, cannot be neutral in the sphere of religion. He cannot remain stationary; he must either rise or fall. If he is lifted up on the wings of religion, he rises; without religion, he falls. A service of the world, which is withdrawn from God, is, even in its most spiritualised form, the service of something which is finite and hence destined for death, even where this finite something is the highest development of purely human spirituality. The cultural pessimism everywhere observed when the things of the world are given absolute value is an unwitting proof of the fact that a godless culture and a pagan cult of pure humanity, however noble, is powerless to satisfy the essential cravings of the human person. Man can be completely happy only when he gives himself to a Good higher than himself, which is perfectly good and holy, and consecrates himself to a duty imposed upon him by this supreme Good: 'Thou hast made us for thyself, O God, and our hearts will never rest until they rest in thee'.

TWO BASIC TYPES OF UNION

The two types which we have been considering so far were only illusory solutions of our problem, because in giving either religion or life absolute validity, they made any union between the two radically impossible. The first requirement in any acceptable solution is an unreserved affirmation both of religion and of life. The most perfect solution, therefore, would call for an equal affirmation of the two in such a way that a parallelogram of forces could be established between the service of God and the service of the world. But this parallelogram of forces, this condition of perfect equilibrium, is an ideal which cannot be realised so long as these forces are in motion. Eternal repose, the perfect fulfilment of human nature in the fullest exercise of the highest faculties in relation to the best possible object, that is to say, in the perfect knowledge and love and happiness derived from the possession and the contemplation of God, is denied to this world and is reserved to a future world.

[7] *Vom Ewigen im Menschen*, I, 512.

We are children of the earth and of heaven, we carry within ourselves the germ of the noble human being and of the child of God, and we must make both germinate and grow.

Now, these two plants, however, stand upon one and the same ground and each one claims the entire ground for itself. This gives rise to a friction between them, a tension or struggle, in which now one, now the other gains the upper hand. It is only in the next life that there will be perfect peace between the two; in the perfect man of the hereafter religion will be life and life religion. This must not to be taken to mean that man must serve two masters successively, (indeed it is indicative of the lack of character of our age that it thinks it can do just this), rather does it mean that while he serves the interest of this world, he does not have to play the renegade towards God, and likewise he can serve God while remaining true to this world.

The state of tension, of which we speak, means that religion and life are torn between two forces, which are pulling them away from each other and at the same time bringing them closer to each other; but the final motive of both forces is always God. Thus because of the fact that the formal object of both is one and the same, there can be no separation between the service of God and the service of the world, and that state of tension is made possible, which benefits and makes fruitful both parts and consequently the whole.

The two forms of life belong together in every age and have a mutual need of each other. They may be thought of as the feminine and masculine principles in the kingdom of God and of the world. They are not equal, but they are of equal importance; and just as human society could not stand without the two mutually complementary sexes, so the kingdom of God requires these two typical forms of life. A living religion will produce them in every epoch. The two types do not correspond perfectly, though one might be inclined to think so, with the two states of the religious or monastic and the secular life, although these are characterised by a more mystic and a more activistic strain, respectively. A very old nun once said that after her death she would like to return over and over again to the world, in order to be able to continue working for the cause of God right up to the day of the Last Judgement. Even in the world there are mystics to be found and even in the monastic life one can find activists. For the world cannot do without the mystic any more than the religious community can do without the activist. One might describe the whole history of piety in a summary fashion as the history of the struggle between pious souls, who were attracted to the world and equally pious souls, who felt a revulsion for the world; this would not hold equally true for the history of asceticism, as the latter has always retained a distinctly monastic note The choice of one or the other form of life does not depend so much on personal liberty as on the particular spiritual temperament with which the person in question has been endowed and on the divine call or vocation, which is made known to him through it. Thus the predominance of one or other type in the individual person is more or less predetermined by the mysterious play of natural forces and of divine grace.

If all men belonged to the same type, then many of the most important tasks pertaining to the service of God and to the service of the world, to the Church and the State, would go unfulfilled, and with the suppression of the tension which generates power, between the two types, a considerable factor in the progress of humanity would be done away with. No mortal man is in complete possession of the unity of religion and life. Each of the two forms of life leads to the one goal; the goal itself lies in the realm of the Infinite. No one, then, can attain to this unity of religion and life; the only thing that is possible is that it can be derived from the divine life and thence brought down upon the earth, and thus divine and human life united in the person of a God-Man. The Church must also be catholic in the sense that she protects and supports both types of life. If we take the cloister and the family as typical manifestations of the two styles, which they only are in a very general way and with certain reservations, as we have shown above, then we see the justification for the words of the English philosopher Friedrich von Hügel, referring to the incorporation of the mystic into the Church:[8] 'The cloister and the family emerge as the two correlative and complementary poles of the spiritual life, both of which have need of the idea of the Church, just as the Church in turn has need of them. The idea of the Church combines the two other ideas of cloister and of family into a state of dangerous tension, which is, however, rich in potential, and it puts the two powers to work in their own respective specific domains. The Church is ultimately the only organisation which is sufficiently composite and at the same time sufficiently strong to give the monk

[8] Reproduced in 'Hochland' XXIII, p. 324.

strength and protection, while at the same time setting up the family in contrast to him as his natural complement, and preserving its own proper spirituality.'

Christianity, which overcomes all the differences produced in men by time and place, race and culture, and coordinates them into a harmonious whole, embraces the two fundamental types with equal love. There is question here also of a *complexio oppositorum*, a synthesis of opposites. The mystic, who renounces the world, has only one aim, and that is to be released from the world; 'that grace may come and that the world may disappear' was the prayer which was wrung from the hearts of the early Christians, as they waited for the Parousia, or Second Coming. The religiously activistic man, on the other hand, has as his aim the perfection of the world by man's efforts until it comes as close as possible to the image of God. The Christianity of Europe has always preferred the activistic type; that of the Orient the mystic type. The latter is in constant danger of falling into pantheism, the former of being transformed into pure humanism. The fact that Europe has been for so long the centre of gravity of christian culture is the reason that Christianity has taken on this marked note of activism; Europe's heightened spirit of work renders it exposed in a particularly high degree to this danger. But there is so much vitality at the heart of Christianity that even in the face of the rationalisation and technicalisation of all human circumstances it is still able to reaffirm its transcendence over the world. Sometimes, however, in doing this, certain spirits who renounce the world fall into the other extreme and give themselves up to an exaggerated pantheistic mysticism, which would make the world dissolve into mere appearances. In between the two basic forms there is a whole scale of intermediate forms, some of them rare and more akin to the brain-children of dreamers, others widespread and effective, according as they approximate more to the one or the other basic type. However, even the basic types themselves must not be thought of as quite clearcut and pure, because mystic repose supposes some activity, and religious activism comes to rest in God. We must now come to examine separately the two basic types of the religious man, namely, the mystic and the activistic.

5
The mystical type
of spiritual life

DESCRIPTION OF THE MYSTICAL LIFE

In every form of religious mysticism the ultimate aim of the human soul is absorbtion in God through knowledge and love. The attitude to life which goes with this aim can show a greater or lesser degree of confidence and friendliness. Sometimes profane life will be restricted to very narrow limits, and consciously made to serve the needs of the mystical life, as may happen in strictly enclosed communities; then again, the mystic may emerge occasionally from his solitude to place at the service of the outside world the divine energies which he has accumulated in his solitude. Thus it happens that within the mystical type of life of which we have been speaking, there are two different forms, the second of which is closely akin to the activistic type.

Pure contemplation

In the first case, that is the purely contemplative life, the world, life, culture are all reduced to fit into the domain of the soul itself; and all the rest of the world is, if not in principle certainly in fact, seen as an obstacle on the way to union with God and shunned accordingly. The greatest possible degree of freedom from the body and from everything material is desired and regarded as essential in order to attain to the true life. The world is not *denounced* formally as evil—the idea of a divine Creation rules that out—but it is *treated* as if it were evil or as if God had created it as a means of testing and tempting man, in order to give himself as recompense to those who would emerge victorious from the test. Why produce cultural values, the mystic would say, if one day they must disappear? Why cultivate the sciences, which can tell us so little, when the science of the saints is far more precious still, and when we will one day be able to see and understand everything better in the divine essence? Why take such care of the body, which will one day be food for worms? Why amass riches which must one day be left behind? In short, why attach ourselves to an earth which can never be our home?

The mystical life was realised at its purest in the anchorites, the hermits of Christian antiquity who, in order to be undisturbed in serving God alone, broke off, or at least tried to break off all contact with the world around them. The recluses of the Middle Ages actually had themselves entombed in a cell for years or even for a lifetime. To this type of mysticism also belongs the cenobite, who lives in a community in which, however, his relations with the other members are purely external; this means that he regards community life merely as a means of assuring for himself a life of continued separation from the world and of preserving him from exterior and interior dangers. According as these communities began to be accepted and became more autonomous, as in Basilian and Benedictine monasticism, so the solitude became the frame for a higher and more noble form of life. In the concept of the 'monastery,' constituted by a community life under the one rule and governed by the principle of stability, the community takes on a markedly different character from that of the cenobitical life. In the latter, the community exists for the sake of the individual, while in the former the community forms a whole, an organic being, in which the individual must be incorporated and to which he must subordinate himself. The result of all this is that the monastic life enjoys an advantage over the hermit and the loosely-united congregation of cenobites, inasmuch as, when it has made contact with the outside world to the extent necessitated by the needs of the community, it can then proceed to shut the door all the more securely against the dangers of its mundane environment, the *claustrum* being a sure guarantee against any penetration by the wicked world.

The three religious vows bar, as far as is possible, the approaches to the world and shut out the dangers which, under the forms of self-love, sensuality and avarice, threaten the kingdom of God. In the religious orders, in the canonical sense of the term, that is to say, those that have solemn vows, the final entry into the order is equivalent to a firm renunciation of the world so complete that the members not only lose their own names in the world, but also forfeit the right to own or to acquire property.

We might think, then, of the mystical life as a great garden, which God divides out into little plots, so that they can be more carefully and lovingly tended. But these plots are of different kinds. The hermit cultivates his own little plot all alone for himself; the cenobite tills his plot side by side with others of the same vocation, but though they work side by side, they do not share each other's work. In fact, in the case of the Carthusian this metaphor becomes a reality, as he tends the little patch of ground in front of his cell while all his brothers do the same in their little gardens; it is in the same way that he tends his soul. In the monastery, however, which has an internal organic community life, we have a larger plot, which is tended as one unit by the whole community, each member being assigned a share in the work, to dig or to plant, to water or to weed, to harvest or to watch. And this communal method applies not only to manual work but also to the cultivation of the soul.

We must remember, however, that the eremitical and the monastic forms are not the only types of mystical life. Inner solitude can be preserved even in the midst of the world and without being attached to any community; and we can find disciples of the mystical life outside the cloister. In the world there are contemplative men and active men and many others who seek to combine the two styles. So too there are also contemplative communities and active communities and communities, which combine the two styles.

There are very few purely contemplative men or communities. The oldest foundations, such as the Basilian and Benedictine monks, come closest to the ideal of pure contemplation. Later communities, however, in carrying out the functions of the Church, especially among the newly-converted and as yet only half-civilised Germanic peoples, were obliged to take on a marked activistic character. The contemplative orders of the Church, as collective bodies, have in the past contributed greatly to the formation of christian culture and are making equally great contributions to-day to its conservation and advancement. In no case is the world simply abandoned: it is simply that it becomes reduced to the limits of the soul or of the small community of which one is a member. The greater this community is, the greater will be the portion of the world which is drawn into the compass of this mystical solitude. In this way, even the man who has completely renounced the world shares in the work of fashioning it to the divine image and so he cannot be reproached as someone indifferent to the needs or impeding the progress of society. A man serves the whole, when he does his share to cultivate a small part of the whole. Again, the man who lives in the community and is cut off by the cloister from the outside world, performs another kind of service to society; besides serving the needs of his own little community, he gives both to the members of this community and to the outside world—we do not speak here of the hermit, of whom the outside world knows absolutely nothing— the example of the perfect inner freedom enjoyed by one who has broken the fetters binding him to a corrupt world. And we have not even mentioned the unseen influence of the God-filled solitude devoted to God alone and never ceases to be a healthy cell in the organism of the Church—influence which like a sub-terrestrial stream or soft dew falling from above fructify the other parts of God's garden.

Contemplation in sympathy with the world

Within the mystical type of religion, we also have a second form, which adopts a more sympathetic attitude to the world; it does not, however, go so far as to regard culture, science and work as autonomous values, but rather sees them as means designed to achieve religious ends. The aim of this attitude is to make as much use as possible of the world from which one has retired, being careful at the same time not to come into any dangerous contact with it. Its motto would be: to separate oneself from the world as much as possible, to give oneself to its service as much as is necessary. The values of the world are appreciated only as means to a more exalted end. The kingdom of Heaven in this world must make use of the means that are to hand, if it is to flourish in the world.

The first type under discussion, he who has renounced the

world altogether, has no great interest in science or art, and
sees his work only as a means of winning the minimum sustenance and of affording himself an interlude from contemplation.
Besides, how could art or science flourish in solitude or in
continual silence without the stimuli and helps given by
society? In the second case we have a conscious cultivation of
intellectual possessions, not only for the good of the individual
soul to begin with, and for that of the immediate community,
but also for the good of the world at large. Science can serve
to defend faith and to smooth the way for it, the arts to em-
bellish God's world; nor are the resources of power politics and
the subtleties of diplomacy frowned upon, when they can help
to advance the triumph of God's Cause. This type of mystic
does not necessarily find scope for his work in a community
only, but the tasks that are implied in his chosen vocation
find their fulfillment chiefly through communal effort. Because
any community is more than the sum of the individuals which
comprise it, and a community can be much more effective
in action, e.g. in the field of charity, than the combined individual efforts of its members. And since charity, in all its
forms, has always been the special domain of woman, it follows
that woman is more dependent than man on this type of
communal effort.

There can be no doubt that this communal approach to life
and to its problems gives rise to a special style of life. For those
who practise it, it is an axiom that the perfect Christian is the
one who is withdrawn from worldly affairs; and they conceive,
or should conceive, the wish that all men would or could leave
the world behind. Nevertheless they find themselves obliged
to occupy themselves with worldly affairs in so far as it is
necessary to come to the aid of their fellows, who are living
and struggling in the world or perhaps caught up in the toils
of the world; in this, they try to disturb their intercourse with
God as little as possible, though some degree of disturbance is
unavoidable. If there were no world, or if the world were to
cease to exist, or if men did not have to be imprisoned in the
body or if men were permitted to leave this prison of the body
then their most cherished wish would be fulfilled. They often
let fall harsh words about the corruption and the perils of the
world, culture, riches and science; and, in fact, one might almost
say that they see this world in the guise of a vale of tears. Their
great joy is when in the evening time or their duties disposed
of, they can retire into themselves, not to recruit their energies

with a view to fresh efforts, but to give themselves up to the care of their own soul or to that of their restricted environment.

To this category belong many religious persons who only incidentally and under duress cultivate earthly values, whether science or education, social welfare or the pastoral care of souls. A philosophy of Platonic stamp often underlies their attitudes. While it does not go so far as to declare the world to be a mere illusion, it does discern over and above the everyday world, another world of reality, of which the former is only an imperfect copy; furthermore, it regards man as a spiritual being misfortunate in being chained to a body, though in a mere external conjunction.

Those, on the other hand, who do not belong in this category, are those who consciously direct their attention to a definite field of activity. They cultivate it thoroughly either as individuals or in community, in order to bring it to completion and as near to perfection as possible whether it be science or education, works of charity or the pursuit of the arts. They are even prepared to sacrifice a part of their independence and right to self-determination in order to be able to devote themselves more effectively to a community which is dedicated to the service of the world and to the kingdom of God. It is this purpose which enables us to class such people among others who are in sympathy with the world, even though they may withdraw from the world into the confines of a small community in order to carry out their designs for the service of the world more effectively. They may wish to be poor in order to enrich others, unmarried in order to serve the community without distraction, obedient in order to devote themselves exclusively to the service of society as a whole. A community also can be devoted to the world, and the individual can deprive himself freely of certain of the world's goods in order to further, by means of an ordered division of labour, the mission of the community considered as a collective personality.

ADVANTAGES AND DANGERS OF THE MYSTICAL LIFE

What is to be said for or against this religious-mystical type? It is clear from the foregoing that it is basically a possible solution to our problem of the union between religion and life;

and in this sense, there is nothing which can be urged against it. There is nothing in its essence which does not justify the form of life demanded by it. It is only in the case of each individual human being, who is the subject pursuing this form of life, that the question of the pros and cons has to be weighed up and resolved. In reference to each specific individual case the religious-mystical type has its own peculiar advantages and its own peculiar dangers, as has also the activistic type. These advantages and dangers vary, however, in the two different forms of the mystical life already outlined.

The world renounced

The first of these two ways, the one which does not condemn the world altogether but reduces it to the narrow limits of its own soul or of the small community within which it lives, can give rise to a unified and harmonious form of life. The man, who, though not condemning the world, nevertheless makes an act of personal renunciation of it, is inevitably denied the rich treasures which spring from the vitality of life and of human society; even the small community in which he lives cannot completely compensate him for this loss. On the other hand, the cultivation of his own soul and the fact of living in community with other high-minded souls dedicated to the highest spiritual aspirations releases for him new streams of interior riches, which cannot be grasped by those, who, however intense their interior life, direct their attention more to the things of the world. If he stands aloof from the outside world, then he knows all the better the world of his own soul and cultivates it with undivided love. For such a one, the cultivation of the interior life can easily take the place of the great world. Renouncing the world in this sense, he dies to the exterior world in order to live all the more vigorously for the interior world of the spirit. For the mystic who lives in a community, this community is the world. He renounces the great world, which, after all, the individual can serve only in a very imperfect way, in order to serve his little community with all the more zeal, and to serve God in it. His position is based on the conviction, so ably set forth by Father Stefan Hilpisch[1] in treating of the spirit of St. Benedict, that 'we serve the world

[1] Kreuzfahrt, Vol. 1, 1924, *Verlag des Grossneudeutschen Bundes*, p. 15.

best when we serve God perfectly and exclusively; that true worship of God is the best way of serving the world; that we serve the world, not when we plunge into the midst of its activities and turmoil, but when we keep at a distance from it and above it. That we serve it, not by criticising it and maligning it, but by making it holy. That our power and strength do not lie in protest, opposition or reaction, but in the adoption of positive attitudes. That we are doing something of value for the world when it can learn from us, not how to build aeroplanes or to assemble machinery, but how to be free from slavery to material things, from war and from the bonds of the flesh. That we serve time when we work for eternity and that we serve man by serving God. That every time we fan the flame of religious life, we also cause a glow of true and warm culture, and that every fountain of purity and truth which we cause to spring up becomes a stream of culture. Finally, that we have as many cultural pioneers as we have devout and noble souls.'

This has been the basic idea of christian monasticism in every age. The monastic life is not the outcome of a spiritualistic conception of the world nor of a dual view of human nature in the Platonic sense, nor is it based on the idea of a world which is evil in itself and a source of contamination to the soul. However frequently it may be misrepresented by those who are outside it and even on occasions by those who belong to it, this form of life stems from the concept, the centre of the Church's philosophy, of the dualism of spirit and matter in the world and in man. The world as the work of God is good and destined to be made perfect; life is a good to be preferred to inexistence. It is not a case of renunciation of the goods of the world being preferable to their use, rather that it is better to strive for the higher values than for the lower ones, not in principle and in a general way but in fact and for themselves. The European and American, who tend to think in terms of work and efficiency, fail as a general rule to understand the mystic who renounces the world. The mystic, in fact, can be understood only by reference to two basic convictions: the first being that humanity is an organic and not a mechanical society; the second that besides the natural ties there are also supernatural ties between the members of human society and in particular between the members of the Communion of Saints.

In justifying his manner of life, the mystic has an abundance

of arguments to draw upon. After all, he is responsible only
for his own soul; it is over it alone he has full dominion, not
over the souls of others. 'What doth it profit a man, if he gain
the whole world and suffer the loss of his soul?' It must not
be thought that it is simply because he is bored by the world
or because he is too timid to assume the responsibilities of life
in the world that he decides to abandon the world. His line of
reasoning is: for me, my own soul is that portion of the world
which has been entrusted to my care. Therefore, I look after
the welfare of my soul, not because it is mine, but because it is
God's property which is entrusted to my care. He who diligently
tills his own plot of ground contributes thereby to making the
whole garden flourish; and the beauty and fertility of my little
plot in God's garden enhances the worth of the whole.

Furthermore, the highest of all human values is personal
worth; there is no other value which can be compared to it.
Every man is a value in himself, simply by the very fact of
being a person. Each person has a contribution to make to the
general good, which only he can make and which cannot be
delegated to anyone else; hence, no man is superfluous. And
every person is of value to the community by virtue of the fact
that he is of value in himself, just as every cell in an organism
is of value to that organism if it is of value in itself. The human
person must not be evaluated in accordance with utility value,
as the world understands it: to do this is to lower the dignity
of even the most useful of persons; in this respect the christian
way of thinking agrees with Kant's postulate that man must
never be reduced to a mere means. It is a fundamental error
and symptomatic of the contemporary upheaval of values,
that personal worth and human dignity are often subordinated
to economic value; sometimes even the economic value is the
only one that is taken into account. Such a system of evaluation
is incapable of understanding the mystical type and the so-
called passive virtues. Nobility of personality is of far more
worth than all the capabilities and subtleties of the intellect
and all the triumphs of culture. 'The culture of the soul is the
soul of all culture.'

It is only when one has a deeper understanding of the nature
and meaning of human society that one can really understand
the monastic type. The monk gives other men, who are in the
world and who only too often misuse the goods of the world,
an example of how to use these goods properly; and to those
who lack these goods he gives an example of how to do without

them without feelings of envy or bitterness; but that is not all. He also prays, works, sacrifices himself and suffers for others. Redeemed humanity, the mystical body of Christ, forms a cellular organism, in which the individual serves the whole and the whole serves the individual. This organism is not a mere mass of dead atoms, but a living and harmonious entity, in which the idea which is immanent to the whole determines the parts, and the parts in turn make up the whole. The man who retires into solitude and into union with God does not withdraw himself from all contribution to the welfare of the family, the community, the State, the Church; in striving to be a good member of an earthly institution, he serves the whole of society. Furthermore, by his outward appearance he brings home to others in the most forcible way possible the finiteness of all earthly associations and he is to his fellow-men a model of a higher family and civic life, that of the family and city of God. By renouncing completely many things which the world prizes so much, he gives others a visible proof that the soul can conquer the material element. By the heroism of his complete renunciation, he teaches his fellow-men to use the goods of the world with moderation at least.

Now, we must question ourselves as to why his works are not directed towards the outside world? It is because his faith is strong enough to convince him that it is not through external activity alone or even primarily that the kingdom of God is advanced. It is advanced to an equal and even to a greater extent by the very existence and nature of religious men rather than by their words and actions, for, whether they will it or not, their mutual interdependence with other men naturally transmits to these others their own strength and energy. There are also invisible channels through which grace can flow; and just as in the physical organism the activity of a cell or of an organ can benefit distant cells and organs, often while bypassing nearer ones, so too, in ways unknown to us, the prayers and works and sufferings of men who are remote from the world can produce at a distance effects which can only be perceived with the clear vision of faith or which are known to God alone. The law of conservation of energy operates also in the economy of grace; according to this law, no energy is ever lost. There will often be an appearance of entropy, of dead heat. When or how it will be transformed into movement and warmth and growth is unknown to us; but that it will be so transformed we can be quite certain *a priori*.

There are dangers, however, in this way of life. The adherent of the mystical way of life must not forget that the world, which he leaves behind, is God's world and as such he must not think harshly of it. Nor must he allow himself to be motivated by an unholy selfishness or by fear of the dangers lurking in the world to withdraw from the world and forsake the task of making the world divine in the image of its Creator in order to think only of the salvation of his own soul. The prodigal son made poor use of his paternal inheritance by plunging headfirst into worldly preoccupations. The elder brother was also at fault however in recognising no duties in respect of the outside world and in merely seeking to increase his father's wealth without making it fruitful for the rest of society. In community life, in particular, this type can sink into a rigid formalism, which thinks only of its own safety and has no thought for erring brethren. The mystical type must keep himself far removed from pride in being one of a chosen elect. This spirit of pride, which looks not only with a lack of understanding but with a certain contempt and pity on the efforts and achievements of human culture in the fields of science, art, technology and genuine enjoyment of life, is frequently to be found but can never be justified.

The mystic, who is endowed with greater spiritual gifts, unless he allows his life to be governed by the principles of a sound philosophy and theology or by a venerable tradition or unless he places his life in the hands of a wise director or of a well-guided religious community can easily fall a prey to subjectivism and to a false mysticism. The history of the ancient hermits and cenobites in the deserts of Egypt shows how the ties with the teaching and the authority of the Church can weaken and how easily a man can forsake the straight and narrow path, if he is in strict solitude and does not keep himself in contact with the community of the Church. Again in the Middle Ages there are similar examples, such as the secret societies, which cut themselves free from the unity of the Church, which had hitherto bound them by authority and tradition, and sought their own direct path to union with God and so they eventually set themselves up as messengers and mediators of divine grace. Through them 'the Church was threatened with the loss of her sovereign control in the religious life; she ran the danger of losing her central meaning as the general form which binds humanity together.'[2] The 'vae soli' of the Preacher:[3] 'Woe to him, that is alone, for when he falleth, he hath none to lift him up . . .' is a maxim which holds good both for the mystic, who stands alone, and in a wider sense for the religious community, which does not remain closely united with the great community of the Church.

Hence the contemplative man requires work, intellectual or corporal, as a counterweight, as a tension which can be opposed to the other force of tension which impels his soul towards God, but which can obscure the fact that this soul is bound to an earthly body. St. Benedict showed his profound knowledge of human nature in giving in his Rule a place of importance to physical work. Renunciation of the world can have the effect of distorting nature, and since grace builds upon nature, an obstacle can be thus set up to the action of grace. 'Moderation in renunciation as in enjoyment of the world, the *via media*, is often the best means of attaining the end for which we strive', says the Indian sage Sadhu Sundar Sing.[4]

In any case, it is impossible to shut out the world entirely. Our very soul is a piece of the world and it shares in the traditions and the inheritance of all the souls who have gone before and who were in the midst of the world: this inheritance from the world is greater than any spiritual inheritance. The mystic cannot successfully till his plot within the garden of the Lord without observing how it is done by those who are in the world; the contemplative has much to learn both from manual and spiritual workers who are still in contact with the world. If he were to be hermetically sealed off from the world, it would mean that his plot would be always tilled with unchanging obsolete methods, with consequent loss of fertility.

Just as no sensible farmer to-day would till his land with a wooden plough, so too contemplative men and communities must avail of improved methods in the cultivation of the soul and make them their own. The domains of the intellect and of the spirit have also got their own laws of development and progress, which may not be disregarded with impunity. In the life of the contemplative, thought and love can be made more fruitful by solitude, yet they bear their greatest and most

[2] M. David-Windstosser, *Frauenmystik im Mittelalter*, Vol. 5 of the Kösel collection, entitled—*German mystics*, Kempten and Munich, 1919, p. 2 f.

[3] Ecclesiastes 4, 10.

[4] *Das Suchen nach Gott*, edited by Friedrich Heiler, Munich 1925, Ernst Reinhardt, p. 62.

abundant fruits within the bosom of the community. Again, those who live outside of human society depend for support and protection on those who remain in the world. All cannot withdraw from the world and go into solitude; if this were to happen, this form of life would be jeopardised, since a world consisting only of contemplatives would no longer afford any solitude and would either have to die or to embark upon a new struggle for its existence. As well as that, we must realise that alienation from the world always needs attachment to the world as a corrective and counterweight, as also vice versa. Without this corrective, there is always the danger of apocalyptic delusions, which can give rise, in the social and political field, to anarchical and communistic tendencies, or there is the danger that nature, having been so violently repressed, will revolt and take its revenge by immersing itself in the pleasures of the world. These two dangers are clearly manifested in the Russian people, who are of a melancholy character and who are obsessed by an over-strong disgust for the things of the world. But a healthy nature and a true culture remains immune from these dangers.

Even the mystic type, therefore, is aware of a state of tension between religion and life, God and the world, spirit and body, rest and work, the individual and the community, tradition and progress. Even when the soul soars up to God on wings of contemplation, it must not forget that it lives in this world and that it is not a pure spirit; otherwise it dissolves in a false mysticism and is lost in the ethereal air of the heavenly spheres. Even in the midst of the highest contemplation, man remains bound to the earth by a thousand ties; we might mention, for instance, that even the state of ecstasy requires the cooperation of the most delicate organs of the body. When these dangers are avoided, this style of life is capable of producing strong, rounded, harmonious personalities, and men who are as perfectly formed spiritually as if they had been cast in a mould. But just as the giant Antaeus was strong only as long as he remained in contact with his mother Gea, the earth, from whom he was continually receiving fresh streams of energy, and was powerless when he was lifted from the earth, so too the mystic, who lives in the regions of the divine, must remain in contact with the earth, and with human nature and its laws; without such a counterweight, the most exalted spirituality will fall into decay.

We often praise the heroism of the mystic, who seeks his

8

path to God by embracing the ideals of the monastic life. and truly heroic is that first great resolve to sever the chains that bind him to the world; the greatness of this heroism is also seen in the daily and hourly submission to the rules of his new life. Not less heroic, however, is the life of the active Christian, who turns his face to the world and takes an active part in all its affairs and enterprises without ever losing sight of his heavenly destiny and without becoming degraded by contact with the goods of the world.

Sympathy with the world

The second form of the mystical life, which takes up an affirmative position *vis-à-vis* the world and which serves it, though only as a secondary duty and as a means to a higher end, shares in the advantages and dangers of the first form; there are a number of new considerations concerning it to be borne in mind however, some favourable and some unfavourable. For one thing, this form of life is not so pure as the first one and can easily lead to a conflict within the soul itself. In its favour, on the other hand, it must be said that the alternation of religious and mundane duties gives rise to a fruitful state of polar tension, which obviates the danger of monotony in the former way and increases receptivity to new and progressive aims and ideas. Despite the advantages of being on better terms with the world and, when organised into a community, of having the power and drive which comes from the pursuit of common aims and ideas, this form of life is threatened by some obvious dangers.

Firstly, there is the danger of a fall from the spiritual heights into worldliness and of the adulteration of pure religious ideals through excessive contact with worldly elements and through the adoption of profane methods and maxims, characteristic of the man of the world. To be effective in the world, this type of mystic, will often be obliged to leave his solitude and the narrow circle of his community; this in its turn can create all kinds of difficulties and embarrassments, which give this form of life the appearance of a compromise. By this, we do not mean to say that a solution in the form of a compromise is necessarily a less worthy solution; we could just as well speak of it as a synthesis. If the ideal cannot be fully realised, and in this case it cannot, since the noble and religious man and the noble christian culture are exalted ideals, and impossible of complete fulfilment, then there is great merit in striving to do as much as possible towards its realisation. But it can happen that the world was not completely renounced or perhaps not freely renounced, and when the mystic comes in frequent contact with it, the world to which he thought he had bidden a final farewell, takes possession of all his thoughts and desires. The world can once again force its way into his heart in the form of intellectual egotism or of spiritual pride or the presumption of belonging to a chosen elect and can give a base earthly flavour to spiritual things. Furthermore, in the religious community one can have a collective egotism wearing the mask of poverty, which is very similar to individual egoism but more painful inasmuch as it is made to serve religious and ecclesiastical ends.

Along with this danger of worldliness, there is also the danger of growing completely out of touch with the world, which is after all, necessarily closed to the mystic. As well as this, in the fields of science, and particularly in theology there is the danger that his equipment may become ineffective, because of his remoteness from the world. No matter how alert and eager to know the world an individual religious may be, if he must always observe it from a tower or only in pictures and images, then he does not have a true understanding of the affairs or enterprises of the world, and he cannot expect to have success when he tries to influence the world. There will always be the temptation to take only half-seriously anything which does not have a direct relationship to religious or ecclesiastical ends and to cooperate in it only reluctantly. He who does not have a genuine love for the world cannot serve it with sincerity and loyalty. The ideals of the religious life and of the community will necessarily require that men and communities, who take some time from their lives of contemplation to devote themselves to tasks which have a relation to the world, will be subject to certain restrictions in their freedom of movement; nevertheless, they must have that measure of exterior freedom, which is absolutely essential if they are to be an influence in and on the world, and they ought also have that measure of interior freedom necessary to maintain that exterior freedom. This brings up the whole question of the tension between law and freedom and again that between inner and outer freedom; we must seek the solution of these tensions in the light of our knowledge of human nature and of the data of experience.

There is the additional factor that the present age has thrown up great problems, particularly in the fields of sociology and pedagogy, which requires the intervention of new minds with new gifts to undertake tasks, which would be beyond the reach of men and communities already in existence. There is much room for fruitful discussion here, as to what degree of necessity there is for this to-day and as to whether the old forms of life and the old communities could not add to their older functions the new tasks, which seem to be called for by our age.

Comparing the two types of mystical life, we can say that life in that mystical style, which keeps itself entirely remote from the world, in so far as it is possible for a life to be entirely remote from the world, is more simple, true to type, unbending and heroic, while on the other hand the life of moderate contact with the world, though it takes from the mystical purity, from inner freedom and profundity, affords greater richness, a more varied formation and the possibility of more immediate action. The representatives of these forms of life within the mystical life can be a great blessing to the rest of the world; when souls come to them, that are weary of the struggle with the world or that have lost courage or hope or even faith itself, they can impart to them some of their own spiritual vigour and tranquillity of soul, which is so hard to come by in the world. The Church will never be able to do without such men and such institutions. There are certain souls, for whom the balm of spiritual contemplation is more necessary than being in contact with the things of the world and who prefer to have a bird's-eye view of the world than to be in the midst of its turmoil; indeed, there are periods of crisis in the life of every man, when he might be counted amongst this number. But it is abundantly clear from what has been said so far that there must be yet another way, in which a state of tension between religion and life can be established by means of a more immediate and trusting contact with life.

6
The active type
of spiritual life

DESCRIPTION OF THIS FORM OF LIFE

The active type of religious man sees the unity of religion
and life in a life which is inspired by religion and which is
lived in the world and with the world. The world, in which the
active man wishes to live and work, is God's world and his
work. He stands 'with strong firm limbs on the solid, durable
earth', but his eye, illuminated by faith, sees always the
splendour of the divine sun throwing its rays over the world.
The tension between religion and life comes clearly to light here
with undiluted intensity, whereas for the pure mystic the world
has diminished and the tension has thus slackened. Just as
God the Creator and God the Father are one, so too the man
who cooperates in Creation by striving to perfect the world
in God's image, is identical with the adoptive son of God in
a mystical communion of love with the Father. This is no mere
compromise, nor even a syncretism, but rather an intimate
organic union set up between sincere attachment to the
welfare of the world and unshakeable faith in a loving divine
Providence; he does not just accept the world as he finds it,
but rather receives it from the hand of the Father with gratitude
and recognition of all the gifts and duties which it brings with
it; he approaches it with trust and confidence and works with
conviction to bring all creation into conformity with the divine
image. In him, nature and grace have become entwined and
harmoniously wedded to unite what is christian and human to

form a christian man. The patron of such men might well be St. Paul, so deeply immersed in the Godhead and in the love of Christ and at the same time so eager to conquer the world. If, for the sake of convenience, we were to call the mystical type of man the Benedictine type, we might call the activistic type the Ignatian, while not wishing, of course, to assert that these two founders or their respective orders are exactly synonymous with the two types of life.

We prefer to call the type of life, which we are now studying, the type of life which is in sympathy with the world, not only in the sense that it affirms in theory the sum total of the worldly values—the mystical type also does this—but rather because it seeks to put them into practice in so far as this is possible. This attitude of sympathy towards the world is possible even when we understand by the term 'world' not just the universe which is perceptible to the senses but a higher reality, which is beyond the world of the senses and of which the latter is only an imperfect copy; in other words, even a platonic conception of the world can manifest this sympathy with the world, that is to say, with this true and real world of ideas, despite the fact that it despises that illusory world with which the senses and the intellect deceive us. It is only when this higher ideal world is identified with the divinity, an identification to which the platonic mentality is highly prone, that this position comes closer to the first type, viz. those who adopt an attitude of hostility towards the world, and may even become identical with it. Hereupon this platonic world becomes a pantheistic or monistic world.

The activistic man who devotes himself to the affairs of the world must always see to it that he preserves the hierarchical order of the values, at least in the sense that he appraises them in accordance with their objective value; even though he may not always be able to observe this hierarchical order in his own cultural work. In fact, the choice of an object to engage a man's special efforts in the field of human culture will be dictated largely by the man's own vocation and his personal gifts and also by the particular needs of the society and time in which he lives.

It is clear that this spiritual activism gives rise to a different form of life, which is totally distinct from the one we have been previously discussing. This form is the genuine type of the man engaged in the creation of a christian culture in the world, a phenomenon which our age longs for so ardently. He is called on not to substitute for the mystic but to place himself side by side with him and to enter into a noble and generous rivalry with him in a fine spirit of emulation. There are obviously three elements which go to make up this style of life: an openness of mind capable of embracing all the things and the values of this life, an unwavering orientation of the soul towards God, a life which is always animated by faith in God, Christ and the Church and which keeps itself continually in the presence of God. Finally, as intimate a compenetration as possible between these two elements. In the logical order, this openness and receptivity to the world would be prior to faith, just as nature precedes grace; in the psychological order, however, faith comes first, because it is faith which makes possible a correct estimation of the values of the world.

On good terms with the world

In its genuine friendly relations with the world, this type can take for its own the maxim of the poet Terence: 'I am a man, and nothing that is human is foreign to me.' This is echoed in the words of the Apostle to the Gentiles: 'For all are yours.'[1] The religious-activistic man adopts a fundamentally positive attitude to all the things of this world and to all its values. He, also, shuns the world in so far as it is evil and tries to keep himself from being defiled by it, because what is evil is not a positive reality, but rather the very negation of a value; the world considered as his field of activity, however, he embraces with his whole soul. This type is characterised by a sense of reality, self-confidence and an optimistic view of life. He affirms life under all its forms, so long as they are true life: nature and culture, soul and body, science and aesthetic sensitivity. He takes up the struggle with the primitive natural forces, within him and around him, and he subdues them and imprints his own image on them, so as to earn the right to take his honourable place as lord of creation. He values personal freedom above all other natural goods, even when, for the sake of a higher freedom, he sacrifices part of his right to self-determination and independence to another, who will be his guide, or to a community as a moral personality, so as to be protected against any misuse of his own freedom or so as to be able to do more

[1] 1 Corinthians 3, 22.

to implant the kingdom of God in this world. He has a passionate love for work, his rule of life being that anything that is worth doing is worth doing well. He works sincerely and industriously for the development of human culture in such fields as education, morality, economy or even simply the betterment of living conditions; and he does this, not because he wishes to ape others or because others have done it before him, but from inner conviction and driven by an internal impulse, a pioneer in his own little field in so far as this is possible for him. And however insignificant may be his contribution to raising the level of human culture, seen as a whole, he is, in principle, interested in all human values. He does not have to be distinguished by any particular talent; moreover, he will generally not have a choice between being active or not. If he embraces the activistic life, he will have been impelled to do so by his own peculiar spiritual temperament or by the social necessities of his environment.

It will be necessary, however, to see to it that there is a just proportion between the talents of different individuals and the work which they do or are called upon to do. Each individual must realise that society has an organic character: that it does not entrust every individual with the same function: that each individual is entrusted with the function which he is best fitted to carry out in the service of society and humanity. In any case, the activistic type of religious man is generally sensitive to the needs of society and to the best way of placing whatever personal gifts he may possess at their service. He serves society and loves it. He never doubts that its cultural level can be raised, even when it sometimes shows a complete lack of understanding and appreciation of his efforts to do so. Not only does he try to smooth away any obstacle to the efforts of the lower classes to improve themselves and to meet halfway their various cultural needs, but he also does all he can to encourage among them a desire for a nobler culture and a more humane way of life. Nothing pains him more than to see men being ground down by the onward march of civilisation, obliged to spend the greater part of their days and of their lives in work, thus reduced to the level of the brute or of the machine, and deprived of the joy of being truly men.

The man who belongs to this type, has a feeling, innate rather than acquired or imparted, for natural virtue for spiritual purity, for honour, sincerity and dignity. He is humble and modest in the appraisal of his own worth, as every sincere man must be, yet he can recognise his own talents and accomplishments without being led into vain self-glory. He knows the extent of his powers but also their limits. He is not blind to the sorrow of the world, but he strives to oppose it with unshakeable resolution and either to conquer it or to enable it to be borne with courage. When faced with evil, however, he is not content with a mere passive avoidance, but strives to overcome it by good. It is here, above all, that we see his positive attitude to culture. He wishes not merely to conserve and heal, but to promote its advance by new and forward looking paths.

The attitude of the activistic type of religious man towards work is a positive one, ennobled and at the same time tempered by religion. The kind of cultural work which creates values is his whole love. For him, work is not just a command but rather a joy and a need. And this love for work and will to work does not derive simply from considering it as a means towards the end of preserving or ennobling life, rather is it a direct expression of his life. He feels himself 'born to work as the bird to fly.' He considers it a joy to be permitted to cooperate in the perfecting of the work of the seventh day of creation, and sees in his call to this work a God-given trust. His mind is perfectly attuned to the most noble conceptions of work. It is for him, in the first place, a play of forces, devoid of utility in the practical order, just as is the primary form of any artistic creativity: It is the expression of spiritual, intellectual and corporal energy and of the joy which accompanies them; it is the manifestation of a deep feeling for life.

Before the Fall this was the only meaning which work could have had, when man in Paradise 'freely exercised his powers, but always with head erect and eyes fixed on Heaven.'[2] Even after the divine malediction had fallen upon the earth[3] and upon its cultivation,[4] the activistic religious man always sought to restore this primal significance to work, in so far as he could. In the second place, he sees work as a means of dominating nature, not, however, for the sake of domination, but rather for the sake of ennobling it, and ultimately of giving it a divine quality. He wishes to impress the stamp of his spirit and of his divine sonship on the nature which surrounds him and which

[2] Max Scheler, *Christentum und Gesellschaft* second half-vol.: *Arbeits- und Bevölkerungsprobleme*, Der Neue Geist Verlag, Leipzig 1924, p. 90.
[3] Genesis 3, 17;   [4] Genesis 4, 12.

is still to a great extent in a state of chaos, thereby restoring nature to the design which the Creator had in mind for it from the very beginning; an image of his own Essence.

The activist, however, is also sensible enough to realise that nature must be subjugated for the less exalted purpose of extorting from it the necessities of life, since nature is hostile to man and only yields under compulsion what man needs for the preservation of life. In this sense, then, work is an assertion of man's rights against nature which threatens to crush the human spirit under the burden of matter. True work cannot be other than cultural work, that is, work which serves towards the cultivation of nature, whether it is human nature with its religious, spiritual and moral, aesthetic and bodily faculties, or nature in the world about us.

His attitude to work must not at the same time be interpreted as a cult of work. He is not what is called the 'Ford-man',[5] who values men only for their capacity for work, the 'homo faber', to whom nothing is impossible and who sees work as the supreme good, who lives only for his 'business' and is unknowingly a slave to it, who forgets his origins and traditions and is completely absorbed in the present time and in temporal matters. It is the great sin of European and American man and one which propogates itself like some hereditary disease that this false spirit of work eliminates or mutilates all other values and that the earthly and the heavenly homes are not distinguished from each other. Apart from the metaphysical and spiritual basis to his attitude, the activist, in contrast to the Ford-man, sees more in the world than just a field for his activity and more in life than just a chore to be discharged; for him, everything is a commission imposed by God, which he accepts with joy and with the security of knowing that all blessing and success comes from the hand of God, whereas the Ford-man has no understanding of anything that is not material and tangible. The activist works neither for the sake of work nor for the sake of gain, nor to distract himself nor to dull his senses against the pangs of despair; rather does he see in work a contribution to the task imposed on humanity and on creation by their own very natures and by the Creator of these natures.

[5] Compare Henry Ford, *Mein Leben und Werk*, Paul List, Leipzig 1924, and Peter Mennicken, *Antiford oder Von der Würde der Menschheit*, Die Kuppel, Aachen 1924.

This activism differs essentially from that irreligious activism, which has long been current in Europe and which is once again being warmly urged by certain philosophers as a means of alleviating the stark tragedy of life.[6] In actual fact, this modern thought is really more pessimistic than activistic. This type of activism is contrasted, as a specifically modern view of life, with the well-defined christian mode of life, which, it is asserted, is hostile to the world; this train of thought is based, however, on false premises, namely, that man, while he may have some influence in the struggle between good and evil, between spiritual and material, cannot play any decisive role in swaying the issue in favour of the former.[7] The contrast between the modern and the christian outlook on the world and ideals of life lies in the fact that Christianity is seen as something which withdraws completely from the world to give itself up to contemplation, whereas the other mode of life is a dynamic idealism, which regards it as its mission 'not only to maintain a devout repose in the world of the spirit, to prepare a temple for it in its heart and to keep its flames burning on a welcoming hearth, but also to spread perfection of spirit abroad in the world and to help it to conquer the world.'[8] Lacking as it does any faith in a divine Providence ruling all human strivings, a faith which is not merely some force in the background but actually governs all activity, this type of activism lacks any firm foundation and is without spiritual vigour and warmth.

Considered on the grounds of historicism, by which we mean a succession of human acts and events not subject to any norms or directions, this activism cannot prosper, since it lacks any deep-rooted convictions. The weakness of modern attempts to justify activism lies in the lack of any *a priori* certainty of the positive efficiency of free causes. Merely to affirm that man can, in the hostorical order, have some influence on the progress of the world and that this makes him partly responsible for the outcome of the struggle between matter and spirit is not sufficient to induce him to stake his life on the issue, especially when a distinct possibility is envisaged that ultimate victory will go to the lower world and not to the higher.

[6] Cf. Hans Rosenfeld, *Glaube und Weltanschauung*, Berlin 1928, Lambert Schneider.

[7] Cf. Alfred Vierkandt, *Der Dualismus im modernen Weltbild*, Berlin 1923, Pan-Verlag Rolf Heise, pp. 104 ff. [8] ibid. 109.

The devotion to the world and to the cause of the world shown by the activistic type of religious man is also very different from a new attitude which, though it goes by the same name, is only a kind of parody of it; in fact, essentially it is the exact opposite of the activism, which we have been describing. Ernst Michel[9] calls it 'attachment to the world as a method' and says that it 'seeks to win souls for politico-religious ends' or that 'it affirms the world as a matter of calculated policy.' Thus, fundamentally, it is not far removed from contempt for and rejection of the world, and is not sustained by the hope, born of faith, of a spiritual rebirth of man and the world. This attitude, which is very widespread in neo-Catholic circles and which stems from the alarming realisation that the ordinary methods for the salvation and winning of souls are making little headway, is obviously lacking in sincerity and integrity and cannot be the way to a christian revival.

Interior Life

This brings us to consider the second aspect of the essence of this type, namely, a living, trusting faith in a divine Providence governing the world, in Christ as God and Creator become visible and tangible for us, and a complete submission to the Church as the community of all the children of God. This faith is not a mere adherence to certain truths laid down for his belief, nor a mere display of emotional attachment to these truths. It is not, therefore, a matter for the intelligence nor a question merely of obedience or party spirit or community solidarity or good example; rather is it something which claims the whole soul and the whole man. This religious faith is not knowledge nor moral rectitude nor emotional intoxication, but the subordination to God of man's whole psychophysical essence; it is this faith alone which gives life a meaning for him. Faith guided by love, gives the spiritual eye a clear vision also of the things of nature and of natural values. There is as much difference between the man of faith and the man who lacks this faith as there is between the man who can see and the man blind from birth. They walk through the same landscape, to the one it speaks of God and of his beauty, while to the other it is shrouded in silence and its greatest beauty is concealed

[9] *Die Tat*, monthly review for the future of German culture, IV, April 1923, p. 4.

to him. Even when speaking of the same thing, the believer and the unbeliever often have something quite different in mind. They think that they understand each other and yet they do not and cannot, since the one lacks the clarity of vision which the other enjoys: 'seeing they see not, hearing they hear not, neither do they understand.'[10] Faith gives unquestioning confidence that God is behind all things and all events. This faith is not something, which is joined to life, but is the very root of life itself: 'The just man liveth by faith.'[11]

The man who has become a man of faith is like a man who formerly saw the world in its own vague light, but now sees it in the light of the sun; for him everything is immersed in God, from his lofty vantage point he begins to see the world for the first time in all its greatness and beauty, just as God sees it. Whatever comes from God who is Goodness itself, must be good because it comes from him. We have the testimony of Scripture that the things of the world, as they have been created by God, are good. If God freely and voluntarily gives life to a free being, then this life must be accepted as a precious gift and not as a burden which one would gladly throw off; it must become for us a task. Even if we have lost Paradise, we still have the Garden of Eden, in which Paradise lay, and it does not deny its fruits to the man who is prepared to work for them by the sweat of his brow.

In circular motion, which is the most perfect form of motion, there is an object which moves at a constant distance from a fixed central point; similarly the religious man moves around a central thought, which is God. This God is not the divine reason of the Deist but the living God of our salvation, not the most real being, as Kant would have it, but the Supreme Good. He is not the object of rational speculation, no mere God of the 'Enlightenment' only necessary to round off a philosopher's picture of the Universe, but rather the fixed centre of all the motion of life, who communicates his own life to the Universe. It is not only the God whom, to use the words of St. Paul, we have come to know, but rather the God, by whom we are known.[12] Faith in God is the formal principle of the activistic type of religious life.

This faith in God has for its object not only a limited concept of the ideal world, as the moderate Positivists would maintain, nor is it a postulate of our yearning for the Infinite, as the

[10] Matthew 13, 14; [11] Romans 1, 17.
[12] Galatians 4, 9.

Romantics would have it. It is not a synthetic theory intended to cover all the aspects of the world and of life nor yet a system to bring unity into the diversity of the world's phenomena and experiences. Again, the love of mankind which is in question is not the detached love of the Enlightenment humanists, which would embrace the millions and offer them the kiss of noble human brotherhood. Both love of God and love of men are founded on the belief that we are all children of God: that all men are related spiritually in God the Father and in Christ, his only-begotten Son,—the centre of that mystical body which embraces all men, namely, the Church. This faith is Catholic, not only in the relative sense that it is the sum of all the elements of truth dispersed throughout all the empirical and historical religions and all the world's various philosophies, both possible and in actual existence; this is how Keyserling would define the notion of catholicity; but also in the absolute sense that it conceives the world and its history as the self-revelation of God and regards Jesus Christ as the keystone to that history.

For the religious man, God is God the Father, as Jesus has taught him to us. In this title of Father, there are contained two elements which are in a state of tension *vis-à-vis* each other: in the first place, there is the relation of complete dependence, in virtue of which we are in God's hand like the clay in the potter's hand, while secondly, the knowledge that we are resting in his bosom springs from our participation in his nature, a kind of blood-relationship, as it were; 'For we are also his offspring.'[13] God is for him both 'the good God' and 'the Lord God', and similarly, Christ is not only the 'gentle loving Saviour', but also the Kyrios Christos, the Christ-King, of Byzantine art, who wears the royal crown, the judge of the living and the dead, with eyes which pierce into the very innermost recesses of the heart, who makes inexorable demands on man and who 'is not come to bring peace but the sword.'[14] The piety, which builds on the foundation of these two elements, combines manly strength with delicate tenderness.

For the religious man, prayer does not signify a deeper breath drawn occasionally by the soul so much as the rythmic movement of breathing itself. Prayer is for him something eternal and uninterrupted, within which interior prayer and contemplation are peak points. The constant quantity in his

[13] Acts 17, 28; [14] Matthew 10, 34.

prayer is the inarticulate prayer of a life and of good works animated by faith; he walks always in the presence of God. The practice of prayer is the expression of and at the same time the means of preserving this prayerful attitude of mind. He does not need all those technical and artificial resources so often recommended for placing oneself in the presence of God, since the idea of God is such a familiar one to him. Just as all artistic creation and enjoyment is unreflecting, so, too, his life is spent in the unreflecting service of God. It is something which is as natural to him as the very air he breathes. He is religious not just now and then but all the time; he cannot, as Newman says, 'be religious one moment and not religious the next, any more than he can be sick one moment and well the next. A man who is truly religious is religious in the morning, at noon and at night. His religion is an indelible mark which is stamped on all his thoughts, words and actions, so that they all cohere as parts of a unified whole. He sees God in all things, and every phase of his life is brought into relation with the things of the spirit revealed to him by God. Every event of the day, every person he meets, every new thing he hears, all are measured against the divine will. Of such a man it can be truly said that 'he prays without ceasing.' For since he is always in the presence of God and since God is always before his eyes, he is in continuous conference with God in the innermost secret places of his life and his prayer, in his humble faith and in his joyous confidence in God. Such a spirit of obedience to the divine will is a spirit which lives within us and guides every movement of our soul.'[15]

The first petition of the Paternoster, that the name of the Father be hallowed, is his first and greatest concern and shapes his whole life. The Eucharist is for him the source of living union with Christ, and Christ means participation with God the Father in the divine life. Hence he brings out the true meaning of those words of the Lord, which are a compendium of theology in themselves: 'As the living Father hath sent me and I live by the Father, so he that eateth me, the same also shall live by me.'[16] His veneration of the saints does not go from the saints to God, but rather from God to the saints, and through them he looks up to God. He loves all the things of the world, especially men, since they all belong to God. This

[15] Przywara-Karrer, *J. H. Cardinal Newman*, Vol. 5: *Weg zum Christentum*, Freiburg 1922, p. 22 f.

[16] John 6, 58.

love is a love in God, an 'amare in Deo', in contrast to the Platonic Eros, which takes exactly the opposite way and proceeds from corporal beauty to beauty of spirit and thence to the idea of divine beauty.

All the miseries and tragedies in his own life and in the lives of others are not sufficient to shake his trust in a good God; and he sees all the vicissitudes of life and the facts of history, especially the fate of his own people, as manifestations of divine Providence, even though their significance may not yet be quite clear to him. For him things do not lose their intrinsic value, but acquire a higher value seen in the light of divine Providence. His work is. at once prayer and service of God. He knows that the struggle of life will culminate in final victory for the cause of God, the conquest of evil, the royal enthronement of Christ and the marriage of humanity with the Lamb in the City of God, as proclaimed in the Apocalypse with such conviction and radiant joy in the vision of the future. All activism is dependent on and bound up with grace from on high, and this is where it differs from Pelagianism and humanism. The holy city, the new Jerusalem, does not ascend to, but rather descends from Heaven.[17]

Religious life and living religion

The salient feature of this type is that the two elements which we have outlined, devotion to the world and the facility for lifting oneself up to God, are not in juxtaposition nor in a relation of subordination or succession, but interwoven in one another. They are not in a state of fusion, but of mutual compenetration. The religious factor is not just a lower layer in the activism of the man who belongs to this type, because if it were no more than that, he would still be leading only a double life, one part of which would remain at the level of pagan humanism, while the other would be in a mystical world and would have no connection with the first part. He would be torn between two worlds and would never achieve a unified personality nor unity of action. He would be no more than a mere syncretism or external conjunction of humanist and mystic. Instead, the two elements are joined together in an organic unity, like body and soul. In the activist, the divine element of Christianity and the human element of culture unite

[17] Apocalypse 20, 2 and 21, 10.

to form a theanthropic being. The representative of this type is the saint in the world, for whom all that is true and good and beautiful is also religious, Christian and Catholic, and all that is authentically human and without corruption or falsification is willed and loved by God. He serves God and God alone, as does the mystic also, but he serves him by means of direct cooperation in making man and the world to conform to the divine image. He is a devoted member of the Church and yet he tries to be 'to the Jew a Jew and to the Greek a Greek.'

In fact, he can do this with all the greater impartiality by reason of being so firmly rooted in the ground of the Church. His is a spirit of virginity in the sense that all his spiritual and bodily energies are consecrated to the service of God in what might be called a nuptial union with God, and he would consider it an act of infidelity against that union to withdraw any of these energies from God's service. He is poor in spirit, seeking nothing for himself and regarding himself as merely the agent and organ of God. He is obedient not only to the will of the Father but also to society and to its institutions, whose demands, whether born of their very nature or dictated by the needs of the moment, he sees as commands which it is his duty to obey.

Men of this type see the world in the light of God, and life in the light of religion. This is not to say that they look first at God and then turn away their eyes from him in order to look at the world, for such a succession would mean separation again, any more than, in order to see things, one has first to look at the sun so as to enable the eye to see other objects. God is not just a *previous* requirement for the contemplation of the things of the world—the *medium in quo*, as the theologians would say—but the standpoint, the *medium quo*, from which the world is contemplated; indeed, one may also have come to the knowledge of God in this way. All the work of the activist is ultimately work for the kingdom of God, which embraces both this world and the next. He does not need to always recall and expressly formulate its relation to its last end; nevertheless a conscious awakening of good will and the conscious exercise of the presence of God can be of great value as a means to an end, namely, that when human weakness threatens to destroy or to obscure this spirit his whole life may be animated by the spirit of faith and of love. The activist will have the humility to confess that often when he begins to waver from his religious attitude to work and when he finds the spirit of work getting

9

the upper hand over the spirit of prayer, he finds it very salutary and necessary to recall by a conscious effort his relationship with God.

The proper relation between religion and life, therefore, is that they should not be independent of each other nor that they should be only loosely joined together. Unfortunately that is how they are related to-day and this is what we feel so unhappy about. Religion and life should not lie beside or upon one another, as one stone lies on another or as one storey of a house rests on another. They are not even joined like two substances in a mixture or in a chemical combination, as, for instance, oxygen and hydrogen which combine to form water; these are all mere external unions. Neither is it a kind of 'personal union', as Elert[18] calls the typically Protestant form of union between religion and life—or what Theodor Häcker[19] calls a 'simultaneity'. Much less is religious society so organised that one part of its members devote themselves exclusively to the world and to profane affairs, while the other part cultivates solely or at least principally the goods of the interior life, a kind of division of labour, as it were. This latter opinion approximates very closely to the oft-expressed view, held for some time by Joseph von Görres, that Catholicism is the feminine element and Protestantism the masculine element in the Christian community; actually there are others who would reverse the roles. The truth is that religious, Christian and Catholic society and every member of it must experience personally this tension when brought face to face with the noble human life and must take steps to resolve it. The way in which each one will resolve this tension for himself will depend on what he is called to; he may turn away from the world or towards it; but whichever way he chooses, he must not deny to the person who chooses to go the opposite way the full right to citizenship of the Church which is the prerogative of all. The union of religion and life can result in a religious life or in a living religion; the union of Christianity and noble humanity can result in a noble Christian humanism or in a nobly human Christianity.

Religion and life are not subordinated to one another; hence there must be no question of religion serving life or life serving religion, or Christianity being at the service of humanism or humanism at the service of Christianity; such service would vitiate each one's peculiar nature and mission. There can be

[18] Hochland XXI, October 1923, p. 23; [19] loc. cit., p. 24.

no relation of subordination between religion and life, between Christianity and culture, any more than the soul can be just an instrument of the body or the body an instrument of the soul, since, to use the scholastic terminology, they are two substances, even though incomplete substances, which mutually postulate each other. Religion and life are autonomous[20] forces which develop in accordance with laws immanent to themselves. Culture, whether in its general aspect or in its specific manifestations, such as State, Nation, education, morality, art or economy, may not make a religion of itself; while religion, in turn, must not present itself as culture. In both cases the state of tension is broken and the equilibrium between the two forces goes, with the result that they are made unfruitful for men. Man is not a pure spirit trapped by chance or through his own fault in the bonds of matter and it is not his mission to free himself from these bonds; neither does the spirit need matter as a kind of stepping-stone to the attainment of its own form of life; in the same way, nature and natural culture are not bound by religion, and the converse is equally true. The fact is that both go hand in hand. Man is perfect only when he is religious, and religion is complete only when in its sphere of activity it has embraced all of human life. Religion is united with humanism just as life and matter are united in the living organism; matter is imbued with life without losing its own proper nature and passes from a passive and unstable equilibrium to an active and stable one, thereby rendered capable of functions which it could never carry out by itself, while life, in its turn, on being united to matter, is raised from its state of indifference into the state of individual existence and is made capable of giving form and a capacity for work to the matter. Religion and life, then, become a single, indivisible principle of being and activity in man. Just as salvation as a whole in its details is at once entirely the work of God and entirely the work of man, and just as the theanthropic works of Jesus Christ are attributed entirely to the divine Word and entirely to his humanity, in the same way religion and life, Christianity and culture, form an inner unity in the religious activist.

From this state of affairs there are two deductions which

[20] It scarcely needs to be pointed out, in the light of what we have been saying, that the word autonomous is used here in a cultural sense, and does not denote moral autonomy, but rather a special structure.

can be made: religion must not be taken up entirely with the
service of culture, whether in matters of education or morality
or in political or national affairs or in economic questions.
Religion is not 'religion for the sake of something'; it must
not be thought of as just another one of the values of life or as
a 'vehicle of morality.' In any discussion of the aims which
religion must serve, one is apt to hear talk of the social necessity
of religion for the common people, but this is a view which is
just as offensive to religion as it is widespread. The consequence
of such an attitude is that religion is regarded as a value or a
duty only by those who need it for the satisfaction of their
spiritual necessities or those who feel that they need it to lead
them to moral maturity or those who find that without it they
cannot keep themselves within the limits of morality; thus
religion comes to be regarded as something only for women or
for those who are passing from childhood to manhood or for
primitive peoples. Culture, then, exceeds its rights in using
religion as a means to further its own development. Religion
may be a necessary condition for creating a true culture, but
it does not necessarily of itself create a culture. The well-
known objection, so frequently heard in former times, that the
backwardness of the Latin countries was a proof of the inferiority of their religion, is based on the false assumption that
a superior form of religion necessarily implies a superior culture.

In view of the close relationship between religious and moral
values one may be justified in expecting that a more perfect
form of religion will be accompanied by a more perfect spiritual
culture, but not a more advanced state of culture in a general
sense, much less a higher degree of the outward appearance of
culture, which we call civilisation. The union of religion and
life must not be taken to imply a suppression of the natural
moral relationships by religion or the Church or by any party
within the Church, in such a way that these natural relationships could no longer have any value in their own right. Thus
the theory of the two swords, so familiar to the Middle Ages,
was a proof of an external strength but at the same time an
internal weakness in the idea of the Church. It is absolutely
impossible to speak of a religious or confessional industrialism,
which would found Christian or Catholic banks or trade-unions,
or of a political Catholicism, by which we do not mean one
which seeks to bring Catholic ideals to bear on political life,
for that is a moral duty, but rather one which seeks to make
political capital for party members out of their religious faith.

The saying of Voltaire: 'If there were no God, then one would have to be invented', makes a mockery of faith in God, if it is meant to signify that religion must serve only to keep the people in check.

The converse may also be stated as the second of our two conclusions, namely, that culture must not be fully absorbed in the service of religion or of the Church. Culture, too, is not 'culture for the sake of something', but it is something which is autonomous. Religion does not need culture, for it shines with an interior light and does not need to be illuminated by science or culture or the State. Religion has need of culture only in the same modified way in which, as we have seen, culture has need of religion, that is to say, as a condition of its flourishing but not as a condition of its existence. It would be an admission of helplessness on the part of religion and of the church as a religious society if it had to depend on the weapons of worldly culture, as, for instance, if it had to call on the power of the secular arm to carry out its own functions. It is only in the case of a complete breakdown in the true relations which should exist between Church and State that the Church could call on the State or on some political party to protect her right to existence and her liberty to carry out her mission. This is verified, for instance, in the case of Islam, where the whole of life is absorbed in religion. A representative of Islam, who has made a close study of the Moslem, states that the main fact to emerge from his analysis was that the political, social and moral life of the Moslem is governed by his religion. 'For the Moslem, religion is not just one domain of life, which can be separated from all his earthly and profane affairs; rather is his whole life pervaded by religion, which guides his steps from the cradle to the grave.'[21] This, however, does not constitute a relation of polarity but rather a state of subordination between State and culture on the one hand and religion on the other. and the fact that the State is a religious institution is the basic reason for the cultural sterility both of this religion and of this State. In the same way, the Calvinist State of Geneva, by subordinating the State to the Church, carried within itself the seeds of its own destruction.

Another factor intimately bound up with this whole fundamental question of the true relations between religion and life is that Jesus in his preaching never sought to recommend human culture. His teaching was contained mostly in the very

[21] Der Leuchter, 1923, p. 101.

simple form of the parable,[22] and St. Paul openly despises the 'persuasive words of human wisdom.'[23] Yet there are many of us who, when engaged in education or in carrying out works of charity, rarely do these things because we feel they are worth doing for their own sake but see them chiefly as a means of reaching those who have become estranged from the Church and of coaxing them back.

There are many who seem to believe that the truths of religion, if they are to convince, must be clothed in the robe of philosophy or of eloquence; others think that religious practices must be accompanied by diversion and entertainment to make them more attractive, just as one coats a bitter pill with sugar; or else they assert that it is a question of life or death for the Church, Christianity and religion in general that they borrow from the State the cloak of authority, so as to assure themselves of influence amongst men. But anyone who judges religion so, has a poor opinion of it. Such people do not believe at heart that the Gospel is in itself 'the power of God unto salvation to whosoever believeth; to Jew first and to Greek';[24] they do not believe that 'the weapons of our warfare are not carnal, but mighty to God unto the pulling down of fortifications, destroying councils, and every height that exalteth itself against the knowledge of God.'[25] In saying all this, we do not mean to deny that religion and culture do in fact contribute to each other's progress and that they derive much benefit from mutual support. For it is on a healthy and well developed nature that faith and grace are best able to build, and likewise culture and noble humanity flourish best under the auspices of religion. Much less are we raising any objection to the use made by pedagogy of natural motives and values in order to exert a religious influence or to the prudent use of profane helps in support of religion or the Church; again, we do not say anything against the use of religious motives for the safeguarding of moral dignity nor against the use of blessings and dispensations of grace on the part of the Church in order to make more fruitful social or charitable work. The only thing which must be guarded against is the erroneous view that religion and the Church depend entirely on these helps and that man left to himself can do nothing but sin.

In itself, religion is neither friendly to culture nor hostile to it, just as culture in itself is neither friendly nor hostile to religion.

[22] Matthew 13, 34; [23] 1 Corinthians 2, 4.
[24] Romans 1, 16; [25] 2 Corinthians 10, 4.

It is man who must be friendly and well-disposed to both, and
very often he does not succeed in doing so. It is true that religion
and culture can be critical of each other in the sense that each
one has a sharp eye for the faults and the worth of the other;
yet the cultural level, taking culture to mean the cultivation of
the purely natural values, cannot be made a standard of
measurement for the religious level, and vice versa.

Religion and life, Christianity and culture are in an inner
harmony, which is based on their divinely-ordained reciprocal
right to existence in an organic unity which is more than any
merely external synthesis. For this union does not remove the
tensions which are inherent to all life, but it is made fruitful
by them. The kingdom of the world is lifted up to the kingdom
of God, and the kingdom of God is brought down within reach
of the world, but neither one loses its own proper being.
Religion and life do not exclude one another nor remain aloof
from one another; religion is not one department amongst the
many departments of life, nor, an essential point, is it just
another department which lies alongside the department of
culture, since both religion and culture are directed to the same
man and claim him in his entirety. Even though the relation
between them is one of tension, neither side sets out to annihil-
ate the other, since they both seek to serve the whole man.
Their union, then, is not in the form of a compromise, so that
each steers a middle course and renounces some of its claims;
no, the union between man and Christian in the Christian man
is such that this Christian man is all of him a Christian and all
of him a man.

Religion therefore, is the perfection of human nature, while
conversely a noble humanity is the perfection of religion. What
Christ brought to men is no more and no less than the perfection
of the idea of man which was in the mind of God from all
eternity. According to this eternal divine idea, man was to be a
child of God from all eternity. According to this eternal divine
idea, man was to be a child of God and an image of his Heavenly
Father and human society was to be a kingdom of God.
Through religion, or more specifically through Christianity
as the divinely-ordained form of religion, human nature attains
its full depth and perfection by being raised to a participation
in the divine nature. The energy which was latent in human
nature but could never be released by its own endeavours, like
the energy latent in a lump of coal, is now released and human
nature is thus made capable of achievements which would

have been quite beyond it, if left to its own resources. Just as the flower of the field, the fruit of the tree and the whole cosmos, organic and inorganic, await the planting and the tending hand and the dominating spirit of man to bring to light their latent splendour and beauty and transform the earth into a Paradise. Just as the rigid and inert block of marble is released from its lifeless existence by the spirit and genius of the divinely-gifted artist and is made to assume life and to express ideas, so, too, human nature by assuming divine sonship, realises the perfection of that which it ought to be by its very nature, taking this to mean its correspondence to the creating and loving will of God, which is the sense in which St. Augustine used it, that is to say, it attains divine life. And it could never hope to attain this perfection of divine life by its own unaided efforts. Thus a new stream of life is sent coursing through the veins of human nature, and once it has been fully imbued with this divine life, that is to say, no mere external contact, then it can never again lose it, unless it makes a suicidal attempt on this new life and thereby renounces its divine character.

Just as he can turn the physical world of nature into a desert, so, too, man can turn the world of his soul into a desert and into a lair for evil spirits. Religion and life, Christianity and culture are related in that their destinies are vitally linked together. Just as the decay of intellectual and spiritual life can often bring about atrophy and decay in the life of the body and conversely an injury in a vital region of the body can paralyse the spiritual powers, so, too, the loss of divine life can bring the ruin of human life in its train and likewise the collapse of a noble humanism can lead to the decay of religious and Christian life.

It is only when life is pervaded by religion and religion by life, culture pervaded by Christianity and Christianity by culture, that human nature and creation attain to the fulness of their being; it is in this sense that human nature and with it all creation sighs for the revelation of the children of God.[26] Far, then, from being suppressed, thwarted or devalued by religion, it is only through religion that life becomes fully and truly life; while far from being distracted or endangered by life, it is only through compenetration with it that religion becomes true religion. Grace presupposes nature and perfects it, it does not destroy nor suppress it. The ancient Fathers, who were more sensitive to these questions of the relation between

[26] Romans 8, 22.

religion and life, between the human and the divine, than we are today, when we are so infected by the spirit of mercenary calculation, sought for comparisons which would bring out the intimate compenetration of the two elements. As the air when infiltrated by light is rendered luminous, as iron heated in the furnace takes on the glow of the fire without sacrificing its own nature, as flour becomes edible only when fermented by leaven, as the wild tree on which a branch of a garden tree has been grafted will produce the fruits of the garden tree without forfeiting its own nature, as matter informed by life will become part of that life without losing its own nature as matter, so, too, man and life when informed by grace and Christianity will assume the properties of divine life without being untrue to his human life.

Religion is not something which is juxtaposed to life, nor is Christianity something which goes alongside culture; religion is true life and true life is religion, Christianity is true culture and true culture is Christianity. Now religion is no mere attitude of the speculative intellect with as little relation to life and the conduct of life as some physical or astronomic theory; religion, as we have described it, modifies life in a completely new way, it leads to a change of ideas, in short, it brings about a completely new style or form of life. This basic change in thought, the 'Metanoia'—'be converted'—of the Gospels, is more than mere contrition and repentance, for these have to do with the conduct of life within the purely moral order, more also than a 'complete revolution of all maxims' in the Kantian sense, for it refers not only, nor even principally, to the moral order but rather founds a completely new order of things and causes a radical reorganisation of life and of all its aspects. Jesus calls the dawn of this new life a rebirth or a birth from on high, St. Paul speaks of it as a new creation, St. John as the seed of God in man, St. Peter as a participation in the divine nature: all expressions which indicate the specifically different and higher value of this new kind of life introduced by faith.[27] It is only through religion that life becomes real life, and it is only when religion encounters a superior human life that it can unfold its energies without

[27] For this reason, the theologians call sanctifying grace, which is the principle of the supernatural life, a 'habitus entativus', that is, a habit, which affects not only the acts nor even the faculties alone of man, but his deepest being and his whole substance and which elevates the entire man to a higher order of being.

restraint. It is only in God that we can see the world as it ought to be seen, and a life filled with God is a life full of value. It is faith which gives meaning to the world, value to life and dignity to human culture.

The man of religious life and of living religion is in principle an optimist, not because he closes his eyes to the tragedy of life or hopes for some chance solution to it, but in the sense that he cannot do other than hope for the fulfilment of God's designs —the best possible for man and creation. If God creates a world, he does not intend it to be a failure, and if he sends his eternal Son into the world of time to plant the seed of divine life there with the purpose of filling men with this life and drawing all men to him, then he must have been certain of success. Whenever religious man comes in contact with representatives of pure humanism, an atmosphere of suspicion and aversion prevails which merely expresses the reaction against what each feels to be foreign and an attack on the other's way of life. Now this atmosphere could be largely dissipated if men of the religious type would only recognise that their own form of life is the divinely-willed perfection of their human nature. Only in a very restricted sense is it true to say that the Christian or Catholic concept of the world is superior to the humanistic pagan one by the very fact of its opposition to the world; this statement is only accurate if we understand by the term world the elements of evil therein. A perfect Christian must not only be pleasing to God but must also have a true sympathy for everything which is noble in mankind.

ADVANTAGES, DANGERS AND METHODS

The advantages of religious activism

The activistic view of life is closer to man's inherent spirit of industry and work. 'God and nature do nothing in vain', as Aristotle is so fond of saying.[28] The faculties of our nature tend to unfold themselves and reach out for some object to occupy their attention. In this way, therefore, this style of life is more suited to the natural and Christian ethos of every age, but in particular to the character of contemporary man,

[28] As, for instance, in his *Concerning heaven*, I 4, 271, a. 35.

in whom the will and the urge to creativity and form-giving activity are so predominant. The fact that this type has not always succeeded in achieving its full development is due partly to the diversity of human souls—some of whom are temperamentally inclined towards repose, some towards action—and partly to the varying conditions of different ages, which have now favoured the one type of person, now the other, according to the alternating periods of creative endeavour and creative standstill. Consequently there have been times in which mysticism flourished and times in which activism flourished, but never a time in which the two views have not existed side by side. In the cultivation of the kingdom of God, Mary and Martha must work together, the one to serve the bodily needs of the Lord, the other to be spiritually served by him; but just as Mary could not always be praying and Martha always working, so too, the mystic cannot withdraw altogether from cultural activity any more than the activist can abandon union with God in prayer. The danger of becoming too involved in worldly matters is greater for the activistic type than for the mystic. And so if we seek to give a simple 'yes-no' answer to the question as to whether the service of earthly or of heavenly things comes first, we must unhesitatingly decide in favour of the latter. However, the true solution lies in bringing the two worlds into unity and harmony as far as possible, so that they now form only one world,—the world of God.

The activistic type is more in accordance with the spiritual make-up of Western man, for whom work is a necessity of life; also it seems to be more congenial to contemporary man, who is more receptive to nature and more enamoured of worldly culture, just as mysticism was more congenial to medieval man. This situation leaves the man of to-day with two choices, either to allow himself to be completely swallowed up in material work or to take this work and to sanctify it. It is worth repeating that to-day as always, the two types of life, the activistic and the mystic, must co-exist. Modern man, using the term modern in its pejorative sense, has a certain inherent pessimism; and although he pays homage to activism, it is generally not from any devotion to the interests of the world, proceeding from an interior conviction, but from the impelling desire to free himself from the suffocating toils of this pessimism; this is the sense of Carlyle's maxim: 'Work and do not despair.' True activism should spring from the primitive energy of our nature, which

was made for activity, and from the divine command to progress and perfect ourselves: 'Increase and multiply, and fill
the earth, and subdue it, and rule over the fishes of the sea,
and the fowls of the air, and all living creatures that move upon
the earth.'[29] It is not to advance the progress of our present-day
technology and economics that the type of person we have in
mind is called; it is rather to take technology and economics,
using these terms in the widest sense, which are so far from God,
and animate them once more with a divine spirit. We do not
wish to obstruct in any way the specialisation of the sciences
or to put any fetters on art other than those which must
inevitably derive from the nature of man and the nature of
art; we do not wish to destroy the factories or to abolish the
complex network of communications between men and peoples,
and even if we did it would be beyond our powers; what we do
want is to put these things at the service of the kingdom of
God and to impregnate them with the idea of the kingdom of
God. When modern man is confronted with his own activities
and efforts and realises how far from God they have brought
him, he is troubled by a feeling of emptiness, which calls for
the only thing which can fill it, namely, ideas and aims relating
to eternity. Our divine Master might have had our own times
in mind when, at Jacob's well, he lifted a warning finger and
said to his disciples: 'Do you not say: there are yet four months,
and then the harvest cometh? Behold, I say to you, lift up
your eyes and see the countries; for they are white already to
harvest.'[30] While some with Moses lift up pure hands to heaven,
others must fight the battles of the Lord. To-day, human nature,
in physique and intellect has reached a peak of refinement
which scarcely seems surpassable, and has thereby reached its
greatest degree of receptivity for the supernatural, in so far as
intellectual sensitivity is required for this ; but now the point
has come where it is beginning to descend from this peak of
maturity and to show traces of decadence. These traces of
decadence will grow more and more marked and will become
the expression of a false superculture, if we unheedingly allow
this critical moment to pass by without making a way for the
entry of grace, which alone can confer on nature the full
splendour of noble humanity.

The religious-activistic view of life gives to life a compact
unity and a sublime inner freedom. Since all cultural work is a

[29] Genesis 1, 28.
[30] John 4, 35 ff.

fulfilment of the divine command, it forms a part of the great service rendered to God by humanity. The individual is called by God's will to take his place in this common service, his particular contribution being dependent on his own natural gifts and on the demands of society. Every such vocation, that is to say, every collaboration in this universal work, is a true service of God, however insignificant and hidden it may seem. The conception of the world as the kingdom of God demands this great common effort by all the children of God. And just as it lends unity to the life of humanity, so, too, does it lend unity to the life of the individual man. Even the menial drudgery which, under the unhealthy social and economic conditions of our times, oppresses such a large part of mankind and prevents the unfolding of its true humanity and which the experts regard as unavoidable for the present, even this loses a great deal of its hatefulness when seen from the religious standpoint as an organic component of the composite effort made by all of humanity to tackle the problems of the world and of our time. Nothing of value—and everything that exists is of some value—is excluded from Christianity. The freedom of the Christian is an image of the freedom which Jesus possessed, and he was the freest man who ever walked upon this planet of ours.

Friedrich Naumann has given beautiful expression to this thought in the following words:[31] 'Each one of us is a slave in so many ways, and this is true whether he lives in a castle or in a cottage. Every one of us has said: I should like to be that which my innermost desires and gifts urge me to be, but alas! I am only the product of my circumstances! Which one of us is not a slave to habits which force him to do that which he does not really want to do? We pace around like animals in a cage. That which constrains and imprisons us we may call morality, immorality, social convention, economic conditions, or, using another idiom, sin, the Fall, tradition, authority; but whatever name we give it, it is always our slavery and lack of freedom which we bewail. It was in the consciousness of such a want of freedom that St. Paul wrote: "Wretched that I am, who shall deliver me from the body of this death?" We wrestle at the bars of our prison, and there beyond in the dim light of the past goes the free man, Jesus of Nazareth, personality itself, freedom from tradition, from the demands of society, from the chains of office; the man of bold courage, who set himself up over Moses,

---

[31] *Briefe über Religion*, Berlin 1916, Georg Reimer, p. 86.

who sat down to table with publicans and sinners, who had no thought for the morrow, a man of inexplicable freedom. To see this man walk through the mists of the past makes a profound impact on us; it makes us humble and at the same time gives us courage. It calls us, to use the traditional terms, to faith and penance . . . Never in the history of mankind has an "I" stood out in bolder letters. If anybody would desire to have a true personality, let him go to him! If anyone would learn not to fear death, to despise injuries, to conquer ingratitude, to overlook slights and false judgements, to bear with sorrows, to work without looking for reward, to give himself without receiving anything in return; if anyone would learn to depose ancient sovereignties, to destroy false piety, to build up new spiritual worlds, to make small souls great, to be in the world but above it, let him call upon him! His personality is independent of all that has taken place since. It is towards this eternal personality that we must turn our gaze.'

The only thing by which the religious man is bound is the will of God, a bond stronger than any human law. He submits freely to all institutions which are sanctioned by God's will. And when others murmur under what they feel to be the burden of the law, he fulfils it perfectly, even when it is only human law, because he knows that it is at once God's law and the law of his own human nature. Tagore has given perfect expression to this sublime freedom in his play 'The King of the dark chambers', when he puts in the mouth of the King's servants, the King being God, the following words, which are worthy of a place in the first Epistle of St. John: 'We do that which we will and yet we do that which he wills.'[32] That is the ideal. It is true that in hard reality there will often be conflict between freedom and the law, because our nature is not yet free and because men do not always know how to treat God's law as God would have it treated; but even in the case of such frictions it is the ideal which seeks fulfilment and which favours the victory of the nobler elements in our human nature over the more corrupt.

This freedom is not to be confused with the freedom of liberalism, however similar they may appear on the surface. Liberalism, is far from being true interior freedom, whether in the field of politics or economics or in the religious and ecclesiastical field. Theological liberalism, in particular, is confused with religious freedom, even though it is, in fact, the exact

[32] Published by Kurt Wolff, Munich 1915, p. 15.

opposite of it, trusting as it does more in its own puny reason
than in the spirit of God, which rules in the soul of the Church.
When the religious man and the man of liberal ideas criticise
any institution, such as the Church or society, they do so from
entirely different motives; when they both take up the whip
to clear the temple, the one does so, impelled by an anger
born of love, which struggles with the human factor in order to
assure the victory of the divine, but the other does so from a
feeling of spiritual superiority, which would put reason and
calculation in the place of simple faith. It is only when freedom
is made conformable to the divine law, which in turn is the
law of our nature as children of God, that the full perfection
of liberty is realised. Otherwise, it would mean only a freedom
of the baser powers and a slavery of the higher powers of man's
nature, and that would be no freedom at all. The man who lacks
this freedom will often envy the (to him) unintelligible liberty
of the free man, and may even be scandalised at it. Think, for
instance, of how St. Paul gloried in his freedom, and how the
brethren who were weaker in the faith took scandal from it.
Such free men, then, must demand more from themselves than
they demand from the unfree and of course, more than the
unfree demand from themselves. This is necessary in order that
their energies be utilised to the full and that they show their
gratitude for the freedom, 'wherewith Christ has made us
free.'[33]

The dangers of profane culture

As well as its advantages, this style of life has also its pitfalls.
They are to be found on the same level as its greatest advantages, that is to say, in the domain of interior freedom. It
can lose this freedom, and forget the warning of the Apostle
that those who use the world should be as not using the world.
A joyous affirmation of the things of creation and an incessant
preoccupation with terrestrial values can make a man get
entangled in those things which are not of God, and this can
lead to a break with God. It can end up as a deification of
culture, science, life, progress, which dwells upon the things of
earth and takes a complacent pleasure in them, and can lead
to a completely worldly spirit, which, taking entire possession
of the soul and driving out God, can cause us to lose the mastery

[33] Galations 4, 31.

over ourselves and over the objects which we should be cultivating and make us slaves to them instead.

Instead of bringing the world to God, we can become worldly ourselves and farther from God than ever. This can be the tragic end of a proud activism, which does not keep a watchful eye fixed on the guiding light of eternity. In the case of the mystic, the gulf between our heavenly and earthly homes can be the means of side-tracking into a false and exaggerated mysticism; in the case of the activistic man, it can have a reverse effect, that is to say, an excessively passionate spirit of work and the power of routine may stifle the soul even of the right-thinking man, and on the other hand, disappointments and the indolence of people, for whom we exert so much effort, can destroy our faith in the divine element in man. Again, for less profound souls, there is always the danger that in the service of others they will forget themselves and become hollow vessels, and while they preach to others they themselves are lost.[34] The ever-vigilant Holy Spirit has to guard the activistic type who spends himself for the world from setting himself up as a high-priest of culture, from rushing in where angels fear to tread, from being busy about many things and rushing breathlessly from one work to another. This type more than any other needs constant self-discipline, without which all his work becomes, to use the words of St. Paul, a vain beating of the air. From being always in the presence of God, he must acquire that constancy and composure in his whole being, which even on the natural level is a guarantee of success.

The religious man climbs up from the natural to the supernatural, and experiences a certain measure of relief at being freed from the bonds of matter; then he looks back at the world beneath him and sees it in a new light, viz. the light that comes from God. As a result of this new vision, he turns back to the world, but not because he wants to leave the higher spheres, for he still remains within the divine light and field of activity, which, however, is now visible to him in the world and no longer as formerly, behind the world. From his personal communion with God comes the realisation that he is a spiritual being with a fulness of personality, and not, as formerly, a slave to nature. Thus God grows in his soul immeasurably, and also a consciousness of his own dignity and of his mission to make the world divine by means of love; and thus he acquires

[34] 1 Corinthians 9, 27.

a goal above all other goals, to acquire divine perfection.[35]

In this return to the world and to himself, the activistic type runs the danger of losing sight once more of the Godhead and of getting into such a position in the world that he is impeded from seeing the light of God's sun. When, however, the soul has once experienced a rebirth and has received the seed of God in itself, then the natural laws of the divine life do not permit it to fall;[36] and if it does fall, then one can only conclude that the seed of God did not take root in that soul.

The greatest danger for the man who is in sympathy with the world lies in the fact that work in general, especially work in the visible world and above all service done to the world in the name of God, possesses a tremendous allure, and many will be found to undertake it without having the deep resources of interior life necessary to bring the work to a successful conclusion. Only a few are capable of this. It is only a soul, which has deep humility and great trust in God, which will be able to guard itself against the blandishments of the world and all the works and pomps of Satan. In the hundred years since their emergence from the ghetto under the influence of Liberalism, the Jews have had to suffer the painful experience of realising that with their emergence into the great world, their ancient religious traditions were a hindrance, and many of their members sacrificed them on the altar of an only half-understood reform. Christianity, too, must learn the lessons of history and psychology. Viewing our age as a whole, satiated as it is with culture, one may well wonder whether it is capable of this interior life. Many of our enthusiasts for a Christian culture would need to turn their backs on culture altogether in order to make themselves more receptive to divine influences and only then revert to their task of moulding culture. Otherwise, they might be seized upon and seduced by the enchantments of the purely human and risk the loss of their souls by a lack of sufficient spiritual strength and preparation.

It is difficult to determine precisely what conditions must be fulfilled before a man or an age can devote himself or itself to the world and to its tasks, without the danger of drifting away from the state of union with God or even losing it altogether. To think that one could live by one's own resources alone without frequent recourse to God in solitude is foolhardy and could be the herald of a serious fall. The world is still a sick world; we are a part of this world and we feel the burden of

[35] Matthew 5, 48; [36] 1 John 3, 9.

10

our animal instincts. If the wickedness of the world is not to drag us down and if we are to cooperate in reshaping the world, then we need to continually revive our spirit and to fortify it with the spirit of God, visible to us in the person of Jesus Christ.

There is something in contemporary culture which is extraordinarily fascinating to the man of sensibility. Modern man, nourished on the intellectual life of the large city, has means of perception and sensibilities at his command far more acute than anything which his ancestors could boast of. It is as though he had developed new organs of perception and enjoyment, which neither the Enlightenment nor the Romantic movement could have had, confining themselves as they did to the sole guidance of reason and intellect. Even to compare the highly-developed linguistic and technical resources of the *Belles Lettres* and of Art with those of the German classical epoch makes the latter seem almost primitive in these respects. Modern man surrenders himself to cosmic life in a way which is basically quite irrational and which scarcely knows or consciously recognises any laws. In the face of this relativism, the traditional restraints of moral, civic and religious-ecclesiastical life are of no avail, unless they are freely accepted and sincerely approved by the man who is in close contact with the life of the senses. It can happen that some modern men feel themselves satisfied with this unconditional surrender; but thinking men will still be able to discern behind this seductive culture the world of the Infinite and will then be more than ever incapable of shutting out the voice of God in their souls. For the truly spiritual man, the ratio between fulfilment and void always remains the same, for the more he comes to value the finite earthly good, the more does he realise the depth and the danger of the abyss which yawns behind him. He who is not aware of the presence of this abyss is in danger of floundering amidst the finite goods of this world.

To be in sympathy with the world is not enough in itself. As Theodor Häcker says with a great deal of truth,[37] 'A true synthesis does not consist in a hasty patching together but in doing a little differently and with more morality that which others have done before us. Rather is it a spontaneous growth, at best when it has remained hidden within us for some time.'

[37] Hochland XXI, October 1923, p. 19.

And however painful it may be to the man, who sees the beauty of this synthesis and who pledges himself to this type of life, to have to wait so long, he will, if he surveys the present generation as a whole, have to agree with Häcker, when he says: 'The work of this generation and perhaps even of the next generations cannot aspire to the achievement of this synthesis; it must be content to work for the removal of obstacles and for the liberation and purification of its own spirit.' In connection with this thought, however, we have to remember that a retirement into solitude does not necessarily mean a flight from the perils of the world, but may rather mean a summoning together of inner strength for the better service of the community.

In an article on the occasion of the twenty-fifth anniversary of 'Hochland',[38] Karl Muth writes: 'It is not retirement in itself which is fatal, but rather that retirement into one's self because of feelings of helplessness; from fear of encountering the world's problems, science, and art; from a desire to preserve oneself from error, because one no longer clings with deep faith to the promise of being the salt of the earth; from cowardice and timidity, which dares not venture on the sea of great spiritual struggles. Self-banishment for the purpose of gaining strength through the development of a rich interior life is not an exile, especially when on our return we are able at once to take our rightful place in our own patrimony.'

Already a great deal has been accomplished if men have been brought to realise once more that the vocation of the Christian is to divinise the world, that is to say, to reshape it in the divine image. Hence it is that those, who already have this realisation, must assume the role of prophet by pointing out this synthesis to their fellow-men as their goal and urging them on towards its attainment. With the recognition of the goal, a beginning has been made to the struggle. To recollect one's own spiritual forces and to inspire the surrounding world are two tasks which must go parallel and not successively; yet for the present the emphasis has to be laid on one's own soul. It may well be that our generation or epoch is too entangled in the life of the world for its own sake to be able to return to the true life; it may be that Europe must first be purged by suffering, as the Hungarian bishop Proházska suggests, or even

[38] Hochland, October 1927, 1, 22.

decline, as Spengler prophesies, or that our civilisation must give way to a new people, who will come out of the East and take over our culture, impregnating it with their own indomitable strength and with the power of eternal life. In whatever one of these ways it may come about, we can never doubt that this final mutual interpenetration of religion and life is possible and will one day come to pass.

The awareness of this danger impels religious activism to organise its energies, especially as the number of those who can be recruited for this type of life is so few at the present time. Community life not alone lends the individual added strength, but in addition, the effectiveness of a community is greater than the effectiveness of its individual members. It permits the principle of the 'economy of forces' to be put more fully into effect, by which each individual can and should be employed in the position best suited to the unfolding of his talents. This principle is observed by most of the existing religious communities of an activistic character, especially those for men, with a resultant increase in their effectiveness for action. However, one could also envisage communities without a *vita communis*, in which the common bond between the members would be found in their common aims and ascetical formation. The members of such a community, would work with apostolic zeal and in a communal spirit for the kingdom of God on earth, at the same time remaining in close touch with the motherhouse where they had received their apostolic impetus. To it they could also withdraw for spiritual refueling, so to speak, for intervals of creative repose and for refuge in time of sickness and old age.

The idea of such a community, like the association for clerics set up by St. Augustine at his episcopal residence at Hippo, where lifelong obedience was promised and all goods were owned in common, where, however, 'the whole ordering of life was based on mutual trust and a consciousness of duty rather than on a fixed rule and supervision',[39] could very well be revived and remodelled for the use of lay-people, who want to accommodate their activity in the world to the conditions

[39] Joseph Mausbach, *Die Ethik des heiligen Augustinus*, I, Freiburg 1909, Herder, p. 352.

of a different age.[40] Thus the needs of our times may call forth new types of communities alongside the traditional cloistered ones. Indeed, it almost seems as though such communities are demanded by the tasks facing the Christian culture of our age. European culture, in thought so rationalistic and economic, in its affections so egocentric, in its actions so power-worshipping, must be once again imbued with religion by Christian faith, communal spirit and law.

This transformation can best be brought about by men, who devote themselves to the same cultural strivings as the children of the world but with the inner freedom of true sons of God. There is question here, of course, only of communities within the body of the Church and in closest contact with her. There is no reason why other trees and shrubs should not be planted alongside the fragrant blooms which now adorn the great garden of the Church; in fact, everywhere there must be a great increase in growth and flowering and bearing fruit, and such communities in all their various kinds and classes must, made fruitful by the dew of grace from heaven and by the blessing of Mother Church, serve to bring man and creation to God. There can never be any question of 'free churches', which are basically only a collective form of religious subjectivism and individualism, just as Socialism is essentially a

[40] We find an approach to this point of view in the rules of certain modern religious communities, as, for instance, in the *General rules for the Sisters of Charity of St. Vincent de Paul* (Graz, 1912, printed and published by the Priests of the Missions), where we read in the first chapter, which deals with the purpose of the Society of Sisters of Charity and the basic virtues which they must practise : 'The primary purpose, for which God has called the Sisters of charity and gathered them together into a congregation, is to honour our Lord Jesus Christ as the source and model of all love, serving him bodily and spiritually in the person of the poor, whether they be sick, children, prisoners or others, who are ashamed to confess their misery . . .' In a later passage, it says: 'The Sisters of Charity do not constitute a religious Order, for such a state would be incompatible with the works of their calling; since, however, they have more to do with the outside world than has the woman in a religious Order and since normally their convent is the hospital, their cell a rented apartment, their chapel the parish church, their cloister the city streets or the corridors of the hospitals, their enclosure obedience, their grille the fear of God and their veil holy recollection, they are obliged to live just as holy and virtuous a life as if they had taken vows in a religious Order, and always when they are amongst the people of the world, their recollection of spirit, their purity of heart and body, their detachment from all created things and their edifying demeanour must compare with that of women in the cloistered seclusion of a religious Order.'

collective and social form of atomism and Communism a collective and social capitalism. These communities must always cling to the Church as a mother and a supreme authority, to Jesus Christ as a king and Saviour and to God as Creator and Father.

The path of religious activism is one which can be taken only by men and communities of a firm faith and great interior liberty. Where they have these, however, they can be the salt of the earth and a leaven for the rest of mankind, the founders of a higher order of humanity, models of sanctity, great and complete men of eternal youth and of unconquerable strength both in action and in suffering. The children of the world gaze with awe upon the figure of the mystic, who has left the world for solitude. For them he represents something strange and inaccessible. They can more easily approach the activistic type and learn from him how a man can live and work in the world without falling a victim to the evil in the world.

The asceticism of the religious activist

From all that has been said it follows that the activistic type needs a special ascetic formation to counteract the dangers we have outlined. The broad aim of this asceticism will be to see that the light of faith and love continues to shine on the goods of the world. There will be no need to depreciate the goods of the world in order to set the heavenly ones apart from them in a distinct light and more attractive by comparison; thus it does not have to disparage marriage in order to exalt virginity or disparage riches to glorify poverty. What is necessary is that it strengthen faith and the spirit of prayer and respect for everything which is sacred. An equilibrium must be maintained between the opposing forces of devotion to the culture of the world and interior freedom, so that the soul does not get trapped in the world, 'the form of which passes away.'

Since it is so difficult to maintain this equilibrium between two forces which are straining in opposite directions, the man who is in sympathy with the world and active in its cause will feel a spiritual need to rest now and then, to put some distance between himself and the things of the world in order to be alone with his soul and with God. The asceticism of the religious activist has not yet been written,[40b] while the way of life of the mystic who has renounced the world can point to an extensive body of literature and to methods elaborated in minutest detail. The ascetic literature available to the Christian in the world scarcely goes beyond the 'Philothea' and the 'Theotimus' of St. Francis de Sales and some gems of advice scattered throughout his letters to lay-people.[41] The Christian who plays an active role in the affairs of the world is aware of his debt to the creators of this monastic literature and method, yet he knows that, for him, these principles are not practically applicable as they stand. Erich Pryzwara[42] rightly says of our ascetical literature that it has simply taken the forms of monastic piety and clothed them in secular garb, and he asks 'if the Christian life of the faithful would not be more intense and personal, if it were provided with an asceticism based on the concrete conditions of its own life?' And he goes on to say: 'The way of life of the Christian faithful is undergoing a rapid process of change and evolution, not felt in the monastery. Are we then to make their religious life subject to an asceticism based on conditions of life which are different from their own and belong largely to earlier times? It is true that genuine Christianity has been essentially the same at all times, but often it is the unessential and the mutable which is the important factor in daily life. If, then, we feel the need to go back to some forms of life which are essentially religious, then we must obviously return to the forms which preceded the division of Christian life into the monastic and the secular, in other words, we must return to the forms of life which Christ outlined for us in his teaching, especially in the parables. This 'being all things to all men' could, we should think, become the keynote and the spirit of a new ascetical literature,

---

[40b] When the author wrote this book, in 1925, a process of rapid development of the 'lay apostolate' had just set in. This reached its climax with the recognition by the Church of a new 'state of perfection': the Secular Institutes. They were recognised and defined by Pius XII in the Apostolic Constitution *Provida Mater Ecclesia* of 2nd February 1947. About fifty of these Secular Institutes have been approved by the Church since then, the first of which, *Opus Dei*, had been founded in 1928. Parallel to this impressive growth of Secular Institutes, an abundant literature has been produced about this life of Christian perfection in the world, as distinct from that in the 'religious life' (Editorial Note).

[41] Cf. Francis Vincent, *St. Francois de Sales directeur d'âmes*,[7] Paris 1923, esp. pp. 217–289.

[42] '*Stimmen der Zeit*', CIV 6, March 1923, p. 453 f.

which could be applied equally to the conditions of life of a merchant or a member of Parliament or a navvy, whereas formerly ascetical literature was restricted in its application to the monastic life or to a type of secular life which, by keeping worldly affairs at a distance, was able to take on a more or less monastic character.'

Nevertheless, the asceticism of the Christian layman must contain a strong element of mysticism. Genuine religious activism always presupposes mysticism, as is evident from the history of all the religious heroes and of all the saints of the Church, from the example of Jesus and of his most activistic Apostle Paul and of all the pioneers and reformers in the Church and from the experience of everyday life. The active man must desist now and then from his activity so as not to be overwhelmed by the diabolical allurements of the world. The contemplative man does not need a similar break because the objects of his contemplation are such as his soul can and may continue to dwell on without interruption. Nevertheless, a physical incapacity for uninterrupted contemplation may cause him occasionally to turn to active work, in fact, it may be imperative for him to do so. In the case of the activistic type of man, however, it is the moral danger of being made worldly by the preoccupation with values, on which he cannot continually dwell with safety, that makes it imperative for him to get away from his activity occasionally. Hence it is that the more profound spirits feel at times the urge to seek solitude in order to enter into undisturbed communion with God and be strengthened thereby.

A rhythmic alternation between interior solitude with God and creative collaboration in the tasks of the kingdom of God in the world, is a law of life for the religious activistic man. The desert is the breeding-ground of great souls; from it have come the pioneers and reformers of all ages. Out of the fulness of the heart the mouth speaks; the heart, however, must be filled by God and he works in solitude. Of Jesus we are told that, after the forty days fast in the desert and the temptations by the devil, he returned to Galilee 'with the power of the spirit upon him', and taught in the whole countryside and in the synagogues to the admiration of all who heard him.[43] The reservoir of spiritual energies in the soul must be replenished when the level begins to drop. Every religious man, but especially the active type, needs from time to time the solitude

[43] Luke 4, 13 ff.

of some Manresa, where new energies flow into his soul from subterranean and supramundane channels. The soul of the activist must be always charged with divine energies, which he can transform into human energies for use in the external world, and then the process, of charge and discharge must be constantly repeated. The divine love which the soul receives from God in solitude is transmitted to its activity for the world in the form of a divinised human love. 'Solitude is a creative interval in the midst of loving, and love is a creative interval in the midst of solitude.'[44] This rhythmic alternation of repose and motion is a fundamental law of life the violation of which will not go unpunished. In the case of the rhythmic movement of bodies in nature, it is not a case of a movement being checked by the movement of another body in an opposite direction; rather is it that the movement dies down slowly and finally comes to rest at a certain point, and then the opposing movement slowly gets under way and gradually gathers momentum. Between the movement and the counter-movement there is a period of repose, in which the forces necessary to start the new movement are gathered together. This creative interval of repose is the condition for the transformation of potential energy into kinetic energy and hence necessary for the conservation and growth of life.

It is this need, this objective necessity, which has given rise to the institution of spiritual retreats, which do not imply any rejection of the ordinary means of saving one's soul but which spring from this primordial law of the alternating rhythm between repose and movement. It is obvious too, that times of unrest, such as our own, have greater need of this repose than times of tranquillity. It is true that this recollection of the soul in God, which is the meaning of the word 'religio', does not necessarily have to precede work in the world; for just as the magnet becomes more powerful in action, so, too, the service of the world and of the kingdom of God, since it is carried out with God-given powers, can bring about in the very act of service a constant revival and increase of religious energies. From the psychological point of view, however, it is essential that a man should be filled with the Spirit of God himself, before he can give this spirit to others, just as the Son of God gave to men of the fulness[45] which he himself had received in the bosom

[44] Fritz Klatt, *Die schöpferische Pause*, Jena 1923, Eugen Diederichs, p. 90.
[45] John 1, 16–18.

of the Father and not of the riches which he had accumulated in the service of the world.

This discussion of the necessity must not be taken to mean that a man must first become perfect before he can serve others; for since he is all his life on the way to the perfect state of active repose, he could never consider himself equipped for this service. The alternation of devotion to God and devotion to the world, of receiving and giving, of repose and motion, of contemplation and action, is a continuous oscillation between two poles. The intervals of repose in this oscillatory movement will be more imperative in moments of great spiritual crises, for instance, in the struggle in a man's soul to discover his true vocation. But they should, in any case, occur at fixed times in the form of spiritual recollection and should recur daily and even frequently during the day. There is great wisdom in the institutions of the monthly period of recollection, the daily meditation and fixed times of silence, so much encouraged by the Church and practised in most monastic communities. But for every man placed between God and the world who does not want to fall a victim to the snares of the world, frequent recollection in some form or another is a necessity. A daily orientation towards God by being alone with him or with Christ creates the spiritual atmosphere, within which the man, who devotes himself to the world, can best accomplish his daily work. Just as the face of Moses was resplendent, as he came down from the mountain where he had been alone with Jahweh, so, too, the man, who has been alone with God in the morning, preserves throughout the day something of the radiance in which he has seen God.

Furthermore, and this is an element which he has in common with the mystic, the religious activist needs a spirit of self-denial and self-sacrifice, if he is to triumph. His very mode of life demands a sacrifice of his whole self. There is, of course, no question of mortification for its own sake, but rather of mortification of the baser instincts in order to achieve spiritual freedom; the surrender of a lower good in favour of a higher. Just as the law of the economy of forces operates for the activistic community in respect of its members, so, too, it binds the activist strictly in regard to the utilisation of his capacities. As a faithful steward of the talents which God has given him, he must not only use them, but use them to the best possible advantage. He must employ them where his own inner vocation and the external necessities of the kingdom of God and of men call for them most urgently, and where he can best serve these needs. Hence it follows that for him the law of the division of labour will be of prime importance. He must not dissipate his energies in tasks which can be done by another with less expenditure of energy; he must not assume tasks which others can do more effectively. Hence, he does not seek out any special ascetical methods, but accepts the occasions for practising austerities and mortifications which come his way in the pursuit of his calling and which are, therefore, imposed upon him by God himself. However, he will also be often in a position to follow the advice of the sage Amasis to his royal friend namely to give up some desired object simply to maintain and increase the spirit of sacrifice, so that God may remain the supreme love of his soul. This would not be asceticism merely for its own sake, but asceticism for the sake of making his love more completely free.

Thus, it is clear that in the activistic style of religious life the mystic element takes a certain priority over the element of attachment to the world. 'Seek ye first the kingdom of God and his justice; and all these things shall be added unto you.'[46] Only he who sees the world as the kingdom of God and who understands that it is a duty imposed upon him by God to devote himself to that world, can conquer terrestrial values. 'Ora et labora' is the correct form, and not vice versa. Prayer, in the sense of turning oneself to God, must take precedence in more than one sense. Firstly, it must be antecedent in time; prayer must be the beginning of all activity; first recollection and union with God, then a turning to the tasks to which our earthly vocation calls us. Secondly prayer must not only accompany work but must also pervade it. Work must be inspired by prayer and must even take on the character of prayer itself as another form of divine service. Finally, the ultimate end of all work in the world is repose in God, in the eternal contemplation of his essence, which in turn is the highest and most perfect activity. Just as on the seventh day of creation God rested from his labours so, too, man, after having done his share to make the world conform to the divine image of it, must take that world or his section of it, and above

---

[46] Matthew 6, 33.

In commenting on Luke 10, 43, St. Thomas expands on Aristotle by giving eight reasons why the contemplative life is superior to the active life (S. theol. 2, 2, q. 182, a. 1; cf. Aristotle, Eth. Nicom. 10, 7–8, 1177ª 12–1178ᵇ 32).

all that part of the world which is his own soul, and restore it to
God, in order to receive God himself in exchange.

The priority of the mystic element lies, therefore, in the
fact that the world and its tasks can only be seen in their
true perspective when seen from the point of view of God. But
this does not mean that the mystic type as a whole is of more
value than the activistic. The active life, according to the
teaching of St. Thomas,[47] comes after the contemplative, in
as much as it is set in motion and directed by the latter, but is
antecedent to it, in as much as it disposes to it. In discussing
the religious state,[48] he gives first place to those communities,
which devote themselves to preaching and teaching, second
place to the purely contemplative and third place to the orders
of charity. Activism, nourished by the fulness of mystic union
with God and placed at the immediate service of the Gospel,
is for him, therefore, higher than pure contemplation and this,
in turn, is higher than the activism which is born of it and which
manifests itself in loving help of one's neighbour. The more,
therefore, worldly callings are understood as serving God by
creating a truly Christian culture, the more they approximate
to the first type of activism and the more they participate in
its advantages. The mystic and activistic types enjoy equal
rights and are related to each other as two opposing poles; and
just as the activistic type must always return to the source of
religious strength and gather his forces anew so as not to be
overcome by the world, so, too, the mystic must continually
have recourse to life so as not to lose all contact with nature.
It is evident, therefore, that neither of the two types can be
exclusively turned towards God or towards the world; if they
were, then the one would degenerate into a pantheistic
mysticism, the other into a godless humanism. Hence it is not
that they have accidental points of contact, they stand to a
great extent on common ground; and therefore there is no
reason why they should misunderstand or despise each other,
much less be at war with each other. Rather must they extend
the hand of friendship to each other in mutual assistance,
striving with noble zeal to surpass one another in their work for
the divinisation of man and of creation.

[47] S. theol. 2, 2, q. 182, a. 4; q. 181, a. 1–3.
[48] *Ibid.* q. 188, a. 6.

7
Profane culture
and sanctity

The problem of religion and life has a particular relevance to the question of the relations between Christianity and noble humanism, between Catholicism and culture. We have up to this repeatedly spoken of religion, Christianity and Catholicism almost in the same breath, as though they were synonymous terms; similarly with the terms life, noble humanism and culture. In actual fact, Christianity is the perfection of religion, and Catholicism is the full realisation of Christianity, just as the noble man is the full realisation of the human being and culture the synthesis of all humanistic values. The same relationship then as obtains between religion and life obtains also between Christianity and humanism, between Catholicism and culture. However, it is not as though noble humanism added something essentially new to man or culture to humanism; rather is it the case that a noble humanism is human life fully realised and culture is the harmonious fulfilment of all the potentialities of noble humanism. In the same way Christianity does not add anything essentially new to religion, nor Catholicism to Christianity; neither one replaces the other, but is the fulfilment and the completion of the other. Since it is one and the same man who is both the subject and the object of the two sets of values, that is to say of life, humanism and culture on the one hand, and of religion, Christianity and Catholicism on the other, and since the two sets of values lay claim to man in his entirety, it is obvious that a compenetration of religion and life, of Christianity and humanism, of Catholicism and culture is something which is demanded 'a priori.' Man attains the full realisation of his humanity only when he is religious, that is, when he derives from the supernatural world the energies which he needs for existence, life and action; similarly he can be profoundly religious only when he is Christian, that is, when he recognises that he is a child of God and lives in accordance with that and he can be truly Christian only when he belongs to the Catholic Church, that is, when he is a living member of the visible and invisible community, which embraces all profoundly religious and Christian men.

The attitude of the individual man towards life, humanism and culture will differ according as he chooses to serve God by serving society, as does the activist, or to serve God entirely and society only incidentally, as does the mystic. It follows from the polarity of Catholicism that both attitudes to profane culture, that which sympathises with it and that which renounces it, in the sense already explained, have always had and will always have their rights and defenders of these rights. Both paths can lead to the realisation of the 'Catholic man', who is the fulfilment of God's eternal design for man. This Catholic man is the ideal man, he is the saint. At all times this ideal of the saint has beckoned to us in the distance, but to-day it seems even further from us than it was in the Medieval Ages of Faith. Modern man seems to have despaired of attaining sanctity, and views the saint as an apparition from the past or as a mere eschatological phenomenon. An essential feature of the Catholic man, of whom we have been speaking, is that he have as perfect a relationship to the world as to God, whether it be the great world in the widest sense or that part of the world constituted by his own soul or personality. As regards life, the Catholic man feels himself a member of humanity and of creation and never ceases to serve the whole of creation and of humanity even if he goes into the desert as a hermit; as regards religion, he realises fully in his thinking and in his life the idea of divine sonship, which is in God's plan the central idea of all religion. Thus, the man who thinks in terms of soul and God alone is not yet Catholic, he must extend his thinking to embrace the relation of the soul with the community of souls in Christ, and even at this, the full picture of the Catholic man is not realised if a third element is not added, that is, the unity of all souls with God through Jesus Christ. This Catholic man can take the two forms of the activist or the mystic, and both enjoy equal rights within the Church.

It may well be, however, that certain periods in the history of the kingdom of God are more suited to, or even demand one or other form of these two forms of life. In one sense it would seem that the present age would be well-advised to withdraw itself from any concern with cultural enterprises, in order to avoid the dangers inherent in an idolisation of culture; while on the other hand, the intense and vital enthusiasm of modern man for the exploration of nature, both his own and that of the world around him, seems to demand all the more forcibly the spiritualisation of these cultural strivings by means of religious energies. Up to this, the man of strong Christian convictions, whenever he has thought about the question at all, has tended to favour the position of renunciation of the world as the one most suited to his nature and ideals, while regarding dedicated collaboration in the establishment of a Christian culture as a venture so risky that he could not see any hope of its implementation as a form of life. But this does not mean that there cannot be an ideal of Christian sanctity of the activistic type. In what follows we shall devote particular attention to this special form of sanctity. From the outline of it which we shall sketch there will emerge certain basic principles of an asceticism for the world, in which direction there have been as yet scarcely any efforts worthy of the name. The saint in this world is the object of the universal aspirations of our time; and this longing is all the stronger in us the more keenly we feel the tragedy of the emptiness which has been brought about in naturally religious souls by an exclusive surrender to worldly values.

CHRISTIANITY AND HUMANISM

The Christian concept of culture

Before we speak of the relationship between Christianity and a noble humanism, we must first be clear about what we mean by the latter. The question is generally formulated in terms of Christianity and profane or mundane culture. And the divergent and frequently contradictory views expressed upon their relationships spring from the fact of widely differing concepts of culture, which often are not clearly or precisely understood. Culture means cultivation for the purpose of ennobling. It stands to reason that the object of this cultivation can only be a positive value; in addition, however, no positive value can be excluded from this cultivation. This cultivation is particularly directed towards the ennoblement of the faculties of man's very nature. Only man is capable of culture. There is in man also a cultural impulse, that is to say, an innate striving to develop more and more his latent potentialities. While all other living creatures are endowed by Nature at birth with every faculty necessary for existence, man alone, as a spiritual being, possesses an unlimited capacity for development. The cultural impulse, innate in him, demands that he realise in himself the ideal of humanity to the greatest possible extent, and in so doing he has to rely upon the experiences gleaned from the past and the help afforded by the world around him. The goal of culture may be identified at three levels; the perfect human personality of the individual, the perfection of human societies and community life, and the progressive ennoblement of the human species in the domain of all the intellectual and moral values. Therefore, there is not only a culture of the individual, but also a popular culture and a culture of humanity. Thus there is no limit to the horizons of culture.

Now since the values which are the object of this ennobling cultivation are of varying importance, a healthy culture will have to concern itself with the hierarchy of the values and will have to arrange its cultural tasks in the order of their relative importance. It is not for religion or Christianity to determine what values the Christian must cultivate and in what order the various possible values must be ranked. It is true that religion and Christianity can throw some light on this question. but it is morality that must decide upon the values to be cultivated and place them in their due order; it must see to it that objects are not accorded a value which they do not deserve and must see to it that a due order of importance is observed in the arrangement of the values. It would not be consistent with the immortality of man that he should create transitory values for their own sake, 'for this world passes away.' Therefore he must fix his gaze upon eternal values and these can only be spiritual values. Hence it is that the chief and proper task of man cannot be the cultivation of the earth or its fertilisation, the technical domination of the powers of nature, or even the subjection of the material part of man's own being. In so far, however, as the cultivation of contingent and material values may be bound up with the pursuit of spiritual and

personal values, then these material values come within the
scope of moral interests and aims. Material values can be
means towards the development of personality, or, at least, a
preliminary condition of this development. Cultural efforts
can concern themselves, therefore, with worldly objects; but
they are not directly objects of culture so much as an occasion
for a condition of or a necessity for development of personal
values.

It is very hard to decide the correct hierarchy of values since
the wide differences between the current attitudes to the world
and to life have marked repercussions in the philosophy of
culture. However, we can safely state that spiritual values
must be put before corporal, religious before cultural and
amongst the latter, moral before purely intellectual, cultural
before aesthetic and utilitarian, social before technical and so
on. But the cultivation of one of these possible values is not
in itself culture. Intellectual formation, moral austerity, the
subjugation of nature, technology, the capacity to enjoy the
pleasures of life, all these can exist side by side without culture,
and in fact, they themselves amount to a lack of culture if they
are cultivated so as to exclude all other values. This one-sided-
ness is one of the chief errors of modern culture. A harmony of
the values belongs to the essence of true culture, as a bird's-eye
survey of the history and scope of human culture would show.
Even in the case of the individual, his subjective evaluation of
cultural goods must conform to this hierarchy. It is to the
credit of Catholic ethics that it has always defended the higher
values against the excessive cultivation of the lower ones.
In decrees promulgated by the bishops of Germany,[1] we read
that 'the bodily culture desired by Christianity aims at the
formation of a body which will be healthy, strong, agile and
beautiful, but within the framework of the formation of the
entire man and with due regard for the subordination of the
bodily to the spiritual.' It is a deviation from what is laid down
by this wise system of ethics to extol the merits of the higher
values against the lower—bodily culture is an example—to the
extent that the latter are completely depreciated or even
looked upon as negative. This depreciation of the bodily factor
is fundamentally irreligious, unchristian and uncatholic. Even
the fact that it sometimes has, or is supposed to have had, a
prophylactic significance is no reason why this error should

[1] Ecclesiastical bulletin for the Archdiocese of Cologne, 20 January
1925, p. 16.

11

be persevered in; for error cannot and must never become the source and foundation of truly noble culture. As regards the question of health and of bodily care, there are prejudices rampant in many circles, which will have to be got rid of, especially in the matter of the education of youth.

The actual cultural work which is most suited to individuals or to groups of individuals will be determined not only by this hierarchy of values, but also by special gifts and qualities or particular vocation to certain cultural aims. The external necessities of social life will also have a large influence in determining the choice. Thus a person or an age can dedicate himself or itself to a particular aspect of culture without violating the law of the hierarchy of cultural values, provided, of course, that the law is respected in principle. For the agent and the chief beneficiary of culture, man and humanity, is a living organism, in the growth of which all the parts do not always come simultaneously to a state of full development, but often do so successively. Thus, for instance, one man can devote himself to social tasks and thereby give up many personal values, either because he does not have any energy left to pursue them, or because by renouncing these values he advances the cultivation of the other value which is more dear to him; for instance, a man can embrace voluntary poverty as a weapon against the evils of capitalism and against the spirit of greed for riches and pleasure. In this way, this man can follow the example of the monk and renounce possessions, family and even personal independence; he does so, however, in a different spirit to the monk, since for him it is only a means or a condition for the better fulfilment of another duty in relation to the world. The ideal goal of culture is the harmonious unfolding of all the noble faculties of human nature in the highest possible measure. Culture means becoming human in the fullest sense.

In view of the finite powers at their disposal which have been further weakened by inherited taints and by sin, men and human societies will always fall short of the ideal of complete and noble humanity. Hence, nature is dependent for the perfection of its own being on the salutary powers of grace. That does not mean that it is the mission of grace, or of the Church as the depositary of grace, to promote culture. However, Christianity does in fact promote culture, in as much as it clears many obstacles which would thwart man in his cultural strivings. 'The Church', says Carl Schmitt,[2] 'exercises an important therapeutic effect, but this does not and cannot constitute her essence.' When Jesus preached of the divine sonship of all men, he was not directly concerned with freeing the proletariat or with extolling bodily freedom as against slavery; however, the higher concept of human dignity, which sprang from this divine filiation, paved the way for the breaking down of all relations of dependence inconsistent with this dignity. Christianity and the Church do not in themselves have a direct cultural mission, but the religious man has a duty to take his divine sonship seriously, and consequently to work towards the ennoblement of his own being. It is only the religious man—we may say plainly the Catholic man, as he is the perfection of the religious man—who can see his cultural obligations in clear focus. As well as the value which they have in themselves, the things of the world have a special claim on the affection of such a man, as being gifts entrusted to his care by God, the Father of the world. The religious man regards it as a labour of love to be able to cooperate with the Godhead in the divinisation of the world. The consciousness of this mission and the knowledge that he himself is the chief object and beneficiary of this creative work must give rise to the most exalted sentiments in the breast of every Christian.

Culture and Catholicism

We are not dealing here with the possibility of uniting Catholic Christianity with modern culture, since the latter is indeed ailing in many respects. Neither is it a question of whether it can be united with culture in general, for, from all that has been said so far, it should be obvious that this is something which can and must be done. What we are concerned with here is its correct relation to culture, the possibility of arriving at a reasoned affirmation of the will to culture and cultural strivings. The whole question of 'Catholicism and culture' has so far been treated from a very limited viewpoint; Catholic apologetics has confined itself to defending the Church and its attitude to the world against the accusation of being hostile to culture, and to trying to demonstrate that culture and Catholicism are reconcilable concepts. That the concept of the

[2] *Römischer Katholizismus und politische Form*, Hellerau 1923, Jakob Hegner, p. 25.

Catholic man implies a reverence for culture and an interiorly felt obligation to promote it has scarcely been emphasised at all. Occasionally, courageous Catholics from the world of science have come forward to assert positively that Catholicism is a principle of progress. Hermann Schell and Georg von Hertling, for instance, have examined the question in writings of a highly polemical character, which have been much controverted.[3] Nevertheless, the prejudice still persists and the fact that we have not been able to kill it is not due to any fundamental opposition between culture and the idea of Catholicism but to the fact that many of those who profess Catholicism are reluctant to believe in the possibility of a union between religion and life, between Catholicism and culture.

Even the most brilliant and convincing expositions of the Catholic position *vis-à-vis* the claims of culture, still leave many Catholics unconvinced. What is most lacking still is empirical proofs, that is to say, people who will combine the two in their own lives; and since life can be demonstrated only by the living, we will never get beyond our present deadlock until men can be found whose lives show a combination of true piety and devotion to the service of the world and of sanctity and noble humanity. For all human development and progress has as its final aim the union of the religious and human elements in the religious man and the harmonisation of Catholicism and culture in a truly Catholic culture.

For the Catholic there is no real opposition between Christianity and noble humanity, anymore than there is between religion and life. They are neither foreign nor hostile to one another, they cannot be since each one lays claim to the totality of the human individual. The religious and christian element is not something which is added on to the human, anymore than noble humanity is something, which is added incidentally to religion. If this were the relation between them, then the two would be essentially extraneous to one another and would soon come adrift from each other. We must not think of God as enthroned at an infinite and inaccessible distance from the world, for the divine Logos is the principle which gives form to all created things and has become united to our nature in the person of Jesus; the divine spirit has breathed

---

[3] Hermann Schell, *Der Katholizismus als Prinzip des Fortschritts*, Würzburg 1897, published by Andreas Göbels.

Georg von Hertling, *Das Prinzip des Katholizismus und die Wissenschaft*, Freiburg 1899, Herder.

over the chaos of the world and has taken up its abode in the Church as the principle of life and of truth. In fact, however, Christianity and noble humanity are bound together only very loosely, and it is being continually brought home to us that this is the great tragedy of our age. Both are directed towards the perfection of human nature, and ought to be united in such an intimate compenetration as to form a single principle of being and of action.

There ought to be a Christian culture and a cultured Christianity. Now since Catholicism is the full realisation of the idea of Christianity and human culture the perfection of noble humanity, Catholicism ought to be the perfection of profane culture. There should be a Catholic culture and a cultured Catholicism. In the sense that it unites Christianity and culture in the Catholic man in an intrinsic and indissoluble unity, one can speak of the Catholic mode of life, both mystic and activistic, but principally the latter, as a 'complexio oppositorum', a synthesis of opposites. And this is the apparent weakness of Catholicism, which is at the same time its real strength, the secret of all its powers.

All truth is contained in the polarity of repose and work, of being and activity, of meaning and of idea. The European generally overestimates the second aspect of reality, the Asiatic the first. In a union of the two lies the possibility, in principle, of enriching the culture of the East by that of the West and vice versa within the framework of Christianity and humanism. The idea of Christianity has been slanted by European man in the direction of activism, while the Asiatic, in so far as one can speak of a Christian culture in his case, has over-emphasised the mystic element. The excessively activistic tendency of the Christian culture of Europe is in one sense a loss and in another sense a gain. It is a loss for the Christianity of Europe as it exists at the present time, but it is a gain for Christianity in general and for the possibilities of its future development, for by means of it a stronger tension is set up in relation to the opposite pole, and this tension calls for the establishment of a state of equilibrium. Now, 'the greater the tension, the greater the energy produced'; in fact, without this exaggerated emphasis on activism, which in this case is really 'the shortest way to totality', we would probably have long since sunk into the repose of stagnation, which is much more fatal than the restlessness which accompanies the struggle to establish equilibrium.

The Christian style of life can adapt itself to embrace both equally and calls for a union of the two; and it is in this union of opposites that the Church shows herself to be truly Catholic. Every unilateral position, every choice of one pole to the total exclusion of the other, is heresy. Catholicism means the fusion of opposites into a unity. That is to say, the idea of Catholicism embraces the whole range of reality from one extreme to the other. In the controversy, for instance, over grace and free will, which has raged through the entire history of the Church and of Catholic dogma, and which is only another version of the tension between Christianity and culture, the Church has always affirmed and defended both elements and has often left herself open thereby to the charge of contradicting herself.

But she has never compromised, never smoothed away, as it were, the jagged edges of the two objects in order to make them fit more smoothly together. She has never taken a middle way, in the sense of watering down the supreme sovereignty of grace or the rights of freedom in order to eliminate the apparent friction between them, but has always been able to confine each one to its own proper limits, immediately it showed signs of menacing the rights of the other. Good is the work of grace and then again it is not the work of grace, it is the work of freewill and again not the work of free will. All that we can say is that it is entirely the work of grace and entirely the work of free will, however contradictory that may seem to one who can view spiritual matters only from a purely mathematical standpoint. The Catholic form of life is not Pelagianism, for which only the forces of nature are of any consequence, nor is it Jansenism, which relies entirely on grace; yet it combines the elements of truth which are contained in both. It is not Deism, which explains the history of the world by the action of immanent necessary laws, nor is it Pantheism, which sees the whole world as absorbed in the Godhead; rather it recognises God as being at once transcendent and immanent. 'Just as the dogma of the Council of Trent does not accept the separation of culture and grace made by Protestantism', says Carl Schmitt,[4] 'so, too, Roman Catholicism does not accept all the dualisms set up between nature and spirit, nature and reason, nature and art, nature and the industrial spirit, and so on. It sees their union just as it sees the union of pure form and formless matter; yet it does not fuse them into something different and higher, a "third element", of which we read so much in the

[4] *Loc. cit.*, p. 23 f.

German philosophy of nature and of history, but which can never be verified. Catholicism has time neither for the desperation induced by irreconcilable antitheses nor for the illusive promise afforded by a synthesis of them.' Catholicism is neither a conglomeration of contradictions nor a mixture of mutually hostile elements, but rather a mysterious union of polarities.

There is no Christian culture in the sense that Christianity has produced a specific form of humanism opposed to other forms of it, just as there is no Christian philosophy in the sense that Christianity has produced a form of philosophy which is different from other philosophic forms; this would be to restrict the concept of Christianity, to reduce it to a means to an end and to make it a mere sect instead of being something essentially original and independent and something which is universally human and thus Catholic. There is, however, a Christian or Catholic culture in the sense that Christianity or the Catholic idea brings out the most in culture and awakens man to a sense of the energies which are latent in his nature and which would otherwise remain forgotten and undeveloped. When a philosopher is a man of faith, his faith does not add anything new materially to his natural reason, it merely opens his eyes to the perception of the real; in the same way, the Christian can be a complete Christian only if he is a man of culture; his Christian faith gives him the power and the liberty to realise the perfection of his nature. Theodor Häcker outlines the nature of the union between Christianity and culture in the following beautiful words[5]: 'The possibility of a Christian culture . . . stands in direct proportion to the vigour of natural intelligence and reason and to the purity of morals, not of the individual nor of a small circle but of a whole race, of a whole people or nation.'

A successful union of Christian faith and of humanistic culture is seldom achieved at one stroke. Generally it is achieved only by those who have been 'born a second time', that is to say, by those who grew up in naive childlike acceptance of this unity and who later, under the stress of serious decisions, came to a conscious realisation of the unity of the two elements. This rebirth is the outcome of a separation which has been removed and it presupposes a faith in the ultimate possibility of a state of equilibrium between the two tensions in a higher supraterrestrial sphere. Religion and life, Christianity and noble

[5] *Christentum und Kultur*, Munich 1927, Kosel and Pustet, p. 50.

humanism, Catholicism and culture are autonomous powers
in their own spheres and are both immensely self-conscious,
yet they are made for one another and need one another,
since they are both rooted in one and the same man. They strain
towards one another and yet away from one another, and they
have to be forced into a union. There are elements which rush
violently towards one another in order to become united: then,
however, their union releases a destructive force which destroys
them both.

Grace and nature are not of this kind; they must first be
forced into a union and a state of tension between their opposing
tendencies must be created. However, once they have discovered
their respective functions and become conscious of their affinity
in God and in themselves, they form a union which is intimate,
strong and fruitful for both elements, which releases new
sources of energy and activity. The man and the Christian
combine to form the Christian man; the man and the Catholic
to form the Catholic man.

The greater the natural affinity between the two elements,
the greater and the more admirable will be their union, whether
in the individual or in society. But this union, in view of its
difficulty, is one which is seldom achieved. How often do we
hear lukewarm Christians or Catholics, complain that those
who live in accordance with the laws of the Church are inferior,
as human personalities to those who know nothing of such laws
or have cut themselves loose from them and go their own ways!
And if this criticism often seems justified, it is due to those who
shelter behind the forms of Christianity to explain away their
shortcomings in the matter of living a really Christian form of
life. The man of discernment sees through this two-faced
attitude, and, in rejecting this erroneous concept of Christian
living, he runs the risk of rejecting Christianity altogether.
Those, who take scandal at a false pietism, may be better than
those at whom they scoff; but they would be still better, if
their natural nobility of soul were united to Christian sanctity.
In any case, the deeply religious man may be indifferent towards
worldly culture but he will never carry this indifference to the
point of hostility, whereas the man who is devoted to culture
alone will seldom be merely indifferent to religion, but is inclined to be hostile towards it. This is due to the fact that the
man, who cultivates the religious values, will generally have
more understanding and appreciation of the lower values than
the man, who only cultivates the lower values, will have of the

higher religious values. 'The spiritual man judgeth all things; and he himself is judged of no man.'[6]

The Catholic and the world

The relation of the Catholic man to the world is no longer felt to be one of simple contradiction. The tension between Christianity and the world remains; it does not eliminate either but rather releases their energies to the greatest possible extent. In their outward appearances, the noble pagan and the fervent Christian may be so alike as to be indistinguishable, but there is as fundamental a difference between them as there is between the lifeless statue and the living person. Similarly, there is no opposition between the here and the hereafter, but both are harmonised in eternal life. We must no longer understand the world in the sense of the wicked world, which is 'full of the lust of the eyes and the lust of the flesh and the pride of life' and into which the followers of the Lord are sent 'as sheep into the midst of wolves'; rather must we see the world as a duty imposed upon us, raw material, which we must form into the divine image, a newly discovered territory, which has to be transformed into the kingdom of God. The Catholic does not approve of the world in all its aspects, especially the decadent and corrupt aspects. He does not fail to discern the sin in the world and does not seek to gloss it over, nor is he insensitive to the tragedy of the world in its many forms; yet he cannot help but love the world and devote his creative energies with joyous enthusiasm to its service.

Besides the world, in so far as it is wicked and hostile to God, there is the world in so far as it is the setting of a new life, which can and must be the fatherland of the children of God. When we speak of loving and hating the world, we do not mean solely that the world is partly good and partly evil, and hence partly worthy of love and partly of hate; the words have a more profound signification than that. The world as a whole is seen to be at once holy and opposed to holiness. The world is holy in the sense that it is God's work and that the spirit of God breathes over it; it is unholy and opposed to holiness, in the sense that it is not divine and that it can fall away from God.

The Catholic must see the world from both points of view. The command of Jesus to go apart from the world is, therefore,

[6] 1 Corinthians 2, 15.

not absolute but relative; relative, in the first place, to the religious subject, who may not be equal to the burden of work in and for the world, or whose particular vocation may demand that he maintain a certain distance from the world, and in the second place, relative to the actual condition of the worldly environment, which may be such as to render it impossible for a man to preserve in it his religious ideals. There are, in fact, certain domains of the cultural life which the man of religious convictions must resolutely shun, though in their case the word 'culture' can be hardly used at all.

In the history of our salvation, the earthly Paradise was succeeded by a sinful, fallen world, which in turn was succeeded by a world which patiently awaited its redemption; finally there came the day of the revelation of the children of God, which brought into being a new and sanctified world, with 'new heavens and a new earth, wherein dwells justice.'[7] In the same way, the attitude of the Church to the world, taken as a whole, goes from the negative to the positive pole, as does also the attitude of the individual soul to the world and to the life of the world. 'For the soul', says Eugen Rosenstock,[8] 'the history of the world is the history of the influences exercised by the soul in the world', and hence he concludes that 'for the soul, the world must necessarily take on a threefold appearance: before they come in contact with each other, the world appears as strange and forbidden, pagan and remote from God, as something to be feared; during the struggle between the soul and the world, the latter is seen as the adversary; while after the struggle, that is to say, after the soul has made the sacrifice of its love, it throws the radiance of its light upon the world, which has received a new consecration and has been restored to its primal destiny . . . Thus before the eyes of the living soul, the world is changed; from being a place of chaos and remoteness, it becomes an arena and a place of struggle, while finally this gives place to a beautiful garden, a newly recovered harvest-field, in which the soul may hope to reap the fruits of its love.'

In the life of Jesus, we find sufficient evidences of his love for the life of the world to be able to assert that he was not fundamentally hostile to the world; indeed, he could not be, since the world was the work of his Father and the scene of his love and miracles. We see Jesus taking part in worldly affairs and enterprises; had he been a worldhater, he would

[7] 2 Peter 3, 13.
[8] Ernst Michel, *Kirche und Wirklichkeit*, p. 225 f.

have lost no opportunity of expressing his distaste for it. He does not forbid fasting, in fact, he recommends it, but he advises those who wish to fast to anoint the head and wash the face, so as to conceal the fasting from the eyes of men. [9]

The attitude of Jesus towards the world is not a negative one. No one can speak of the things of the world with such love as he does if he despises them at heart, and in fact, many of our modern ascetics can find no support in the life and words of Jesus for their condemnations of the world. When he spoke of authority,[10] power,[11] the State,[12] sovereignty,[13] he did so with a serenity and matter-of-factness, which rule out any idea that he could have regarded them as obstacles to salvation. If he had despised the world, he would not have failed to seize every opportunity to proclaim his hatred of it, as does the Preacher of the Bible and likewise many of those who preach Christianity in our time.

In the case of John the Baptist, the retreat from the world stemmed from the conviction that the axe was laid to the root of the tree, that the world was heading for destruction and could no longer be saved, and that the kingdom of God could be built up only on the ruins of the world which had existed up to that time. For Jesus, however, the reconstruction of the world would not come by way of a catastrophe nor by the abolition of the law and the prophets, but by their fulfilment. For him, also, there is an opposition between the new and the old world, justifying an attitude of hate for the world and a determination to fly it. It is not a radical and absolute opposition, but conditional and factual. For him, this hatred of the world is to be the means to the renovation of the already existing world. We must hate what is evil in the world, in order to bring about the triumph of the good and in order to make the world worthy once more of the divine love. The divine in the world has been, as it were, roughly hewn out by God; it is for man to seek out these roughly traced outlines and to carve and polish them.

Even Original Sin and all its consequences has not been able to efface these rough outlines of the divine in the world. The Catholic no longer seeks a Paradise beyond the stars, he knows that there is a kingdom of God on this earth. In fact, God himself took man and set him in the garden of Eden, to till and tend it; he even commanded him to eat of the trees in the

---

[9] Matthew 6, 16–18; [10] Matthew 20, 25; [11] Luke 19, 17.
[12] Matthew 22, 21; [13] Luke 7, 8.

garden, and made him the permanent tenant of the earth by
giving him a companion, who was like unto himself.[14] 'The
heaven of heaven is the Lord's: but the earth he has given to
the children of men.'[15] The man who realises these things
accepts the gifts of nature and the joys of life with gratitude
from the hand of God, for 'the earth is the Lord's and the fulness
thereof',[16] and therefore, they are good just as God is good.
'For all are yours; and you are Christ's; and Christ is God's.'[17]
Therefore, one must not take the world to mean simply the
world, in so far as it is evil, any more than one may understand
profane science as a science, which is necessarily opposed to
faith or profane culture as necessarily a false culture. The world
may, in some respects, be an object of aversion, but it is also
the object of God's love, 'For God so loved the world, as to
give his only-begotten Son; that whosoever believeth in him,
may not perish but may have life everlasting.' And this his
son he has sent, not to judge the world, but that the world
might be saved by him.[18] The world, in which Jesus has walked,
is sanctified and designed for saints.

The activistic type of religious man is not unaware of the
tragic elements in human existence; in fact, he sees them more
clearly and feels them more keenly than other men, because
he realises more clearly man's true destiny as an image of the
divine and a second Christ, and consequently realises how
impossible it is for human life to measure up to its sublime
dignity. The finite nature of our being, the sinfulness of his
own soul and the degradation of mankind are a source of
constant torment to him, and keep him from ever regarding
life as one unqualified joy. Nevertheless, the greater the tragedy
of life and the more it causes him to suffer, the more does he
have confidence that this tragedy will one day be resolved in
peace and joy; his constant sorrow at the tardy coming of the
kingdom of God keeps him from being overwhelmed by lesser
disappointments and sorrows in life, such as the death of loved
ones, which are often a source of uncontrollable grief to others.
In fact, he will sometimes be rather amazed and embarrassed
at finding himself incapable of the great compassion which
others feel at these times and expect him to feel, too, and at
being unable to feel the tragedy in things which cause other
hearts to bleed. But no other crosses can weigh upon him as

[14] Genesis 2, 15 ff.; [15] Ps. 113, 16.
[16] 1 Corinthians 10, 26; [17] 1 Corinthians 3, 22 f.
[18] John 3, 15–17.

heavily as the weakness and the sinfulness of his own soul and of the society to which he feels himself bound.

Far from being drawn into a hopeless rebellion against the cross by an exaggerated notion of his own powers, he bows humbly under the cross and under the hand of God which imposes it, not, however, with that sullen resignation with which many others, whose faith is weak, accept it as an inevitable fate. This pessimistic passivity gives place, in his case, to an active outlook; the cross becomes 'a safe ladder, by which one ascends to life.' The Christian sufferer is very far removed from that stoic impassivity which despises all sorrow and argues away the existence of sin and evil with sophistic self-deceptions. He will often find himself in danger of being led astray by the world and by his own inclinations, but he will steadily resist this, seeing in it a lack of confidence in God and a temptation against faith, which, if he were to yield to it for any length of time, would be equivalent to a betrayal of his very nature.

Even in the life of Jesus there are no real tragic moments. He lived a life of perfect conformity with the will of his heavenly Father, and therefore perfect peace reigned in the very profoundest depths of his being. Even when his Passion, the sufferings of which he had clearly foreseen, burst like a torrent upon his head, 'he rejoiced, like a giant, to run the course.' It has been truly said that, for the Christian dramatist, there can be no such thing as tragedy because, with the penetration of vision which his faith in a divine Providence gives him, the Christian is able to discern behind every apparent tragedy a happy solution of the conflict. Hence, though his hero may succumb in the struggle, his ideas and thus his better self must always emerge victorious.

The unity of Christianity and noble humanism is the best apologia for both sides. The many objections made against Christianity in particular, would be silenced if its defenders could point to a noble culture within it or to a large number of Christians who consciously recognised the union of the two elements as a duty and earnestly sought after it and achieved it to some extent. Christian apologetics must continue to defend the truth of their ideas and the superiority of their principles of life, but it would have a very welcome proof of the truth of these ideas if it could point to their concrete fulfilment in the Christian man. And after all, it is only to be expected that in the Christian man a higher development of his purely human personality will be apparent than in non-

Christian. We rejoice so much in the truth of our religion and pride ourselves upon it; if we could only rejoice also in the realisation in ourselves of that unity, which the world of to-day needs so badly! Take, for instance, the many different organisations which are working for the reunion of the Christian churches: how much more effective and promising their work would be amongst those who are seeking for the true Church if their doctrinal teaching were backed up by the example of a true culture, based on the spirit of Christianity! The Church would be in a position to make tremendous conquests, if it could visibly represent in a large number of its members that beautiful harmony of the Christian life and the noble human life. It should no longer be a cause of wonder for a prominent personage in public life not only to profess Catholicism but also to live by it and draw his strength from it. The fact that such a phenomenon never fails to produce expressions of surprise is a proof of how little it is realised by people in general that Christianity and noble humanity are two values which complement each other and have a mutual need of each other.

But there can be no hope of the establishment of a Christian culture until the Catholic of our time changes his basic thinking, which is very different from that of the Church as a whole, to arrive at a more positive *rapprochement* with the duties imposed by culture in all its diverse spheres, whether it be science or art or technology or economy or whatever else it may be. His reserve in this matter springs from a sort of delicate sixth sense, which warns the Catholic of the dangers lurking in cultural endeavours and the false elements in our modern civilisation; nevertheless, it cannot be justified on these grounds. The efforts, which we have been making, to defend ourselves against the reproaches of cultural backwardness have had their origin in a mere half-hearted confidence in our own powers and hence they have awakened only a half-hearted response. Of course, not everyone is entrusted with this mission; many will be called to the state of life of the mystic. However, those who have this mission must embrace it with enthusiasm and an unshakeable faith in the possibility of a deification of the world in Christ through the grace of God. The belief or the feeling that the organic union of religion and life in general and of Christianity and noble humanism in particular is the only means of preserving the Christian civilisation of Europe has been winning favour amongst many far-seeing thinkers, many of them even outside of Christianity.

After the terrible calamities brought upon the world by the last war, the view has been gaining ground that only a harmonious compenetration of culture with Christian ideas can save the world from another cataclysm. And hence it is that even culture itself seeks this union with, and also the support of, the Catholic Church. 'To-day', says Count Hermann Keyserling,[19] 'the leading figures of all creeds are striving to establish a universal Christianity, which will embrace all men and creeds; they all feel that the point in history has come when the hour strikes for an oecumenical Christianity, and it is only natural that each one should hope that his own particular creed will be the basis of this universal religion', But mankind can be thus satisfied only by a Christianity, which is not merely international but supranational, and human in the very broadest sense of the word, that is to say, Catholic. At the meeting of the Society for free Philosophy in Darmstadt in Autumn of the year 1923, the theme 'Ideas of the world and of the ordering of life'; was discussed and Keyserling sums up the result of this discussion by saying that it was unanimously agreed that 'the Catholic Church, considered as a form of expression of Christian thought, represents the highest form of unity, and assimilates into its own being all that is worth preserving in humanity's conception of the world and its approach to the conduct of life.'[20] This is something which, he says, the Greek Orthodox Church could not do, since its very essence is unhistoric, even anti-historic, and consequently it could never measure up to an historic task or produce a new historic form; neither could the Protestant Church, since it is still largely movement and has not taken on fixed stable form to any significant extent; besides, it has completed its historical mission.

The Catholic Church is, however, by its very essence the universal Christian Church and it alone contains in principle all the manifestations of Christian life. Yet Keyserling immediately goes on to say that, although the Catholic Church is the only one which can realise this unifying mission, there are many factors which are unfavourable to this mission in her present-day make-up, in particular, the defensive attitude into which she was forced by the Reformation; and he goes on to predict that 'unless she measures up to the demands of our epoch, as she was well able to do before being forced into a defensive position by the Reformation', her decline will come

[19] *Der Leuchter*, 1924, p. 263; [20] ibid., 265.

about. He believes, furthermore, that even if she succeeds in uniting all Christianity, she will never be able to embrace the whole of mankind, since she is still only the religion of the West; the oecumenical Christianity of the future, he says, can not proceed from a synthesis of all the present-day creeds but from the struggle between them, it will not be the result of an artificial syncretism, arrived at by way of compromise and concession, but will be the result of a rebirth. However much this view may be open to criticism, it has a kernel of truth, namely, that Europe and the world can look only to the Catholic to preserve her culture and to give her new cultural life. The goal of an ennobled humanity, cannot be attained by nature, when it is left to its own devices. Christianity may not be the means, but it is an essential condition for the attainment of this goal.

Our present age is in much the same situation as the world of Greek culture when the Macedonian appeared in a dream to St. Paul and begged him: 'Come over and help us.' One would need to close one's eyes completely to the restless stirrings of our times to be unaware of the longing which haunts contemporary civilisation for the unknown God. That is not to say, however, that we are to think in terms of mass conversions, or that we are to entertain visions of contemporary philosophy marching back into the camp of the Church with banners flying. We can state quite definitely in advance that this will not happen. However, the disquietude and the uncertainty, so widespread outside the Church and outside Christianity, is already one of the negative conditions for a return to Christian culture.

The union of religion and life was more easily attained at a time when the Church had to regard the promotion of cultural aims as her own concern, partly because she wanted to build a solid foundation for grace and partly because the State had not yet become so powerful as to be able to take upon itself the advancement of all the material interests of a Christian society. Now, however, when the State, fully conscious of its own power and maturity, has taken these cultural interests out of the hands of the Church and has adopted an attitude of indifference and even of hostility to the Church, it is inevitable that a certain amount of friction and contradiction has crept in between its conception of culture and that of Christianity. Catholics, generally, advocate the claims of tradition, and do so very successfully. This is one of the reasons for the formidable power of the Church, since in this territory she moves with a firm front and with unshakeable security; towards what is new, however, she is reserved and sceptical.

Hence it is that the Catholic Church is always to the fore when there is question of combating erroneous ideas or danger-ous innovations, but unfortunately her conservatism holds her back when it comes to taking up a position of leadership and assuming the initiative in creative work and progressive ventures. She is too easily made to take second place and pushed into the background, and then, when she does lend her cooperation, she is made to look an unwilling partner, tolerated rather than readily accepted. Now, it must be the aim of the Church to imbue the institutions of the State and of society with her own spirit; and this she must do from below and from within. In other words she must do this not by her own solid impact as a society but by the influence of her in-dividual members. Then Europe and the world would become Christian for the second time, and be more Christian at heart this time than ever before. And one day, too, the State would realise with astonishment that, through the Christian spirit of its citizens, it had itself become Christian.

The culture of our age, which is so proud of its successes, and rightly so, but which without a proper relation to religion lacks its deepest meaning, must be persuaded that it does not need to forfeit any of its conquests, but can bring them all along with it into the temple of religion, and that in fact, these cultural possessions will glow more beautifully and resplendently than ever before, when illuminated by the seven-branched candle-stick of the faith. For it is this mistaken idea that anyone who professes Christianity must renounce completely everything profane that has nurtured the separation which concerns us so much.

A Christian culture or Catholic humanism is, then, an ideal. We do not expect the kingdom of God to come in our time, since it is not fully realised in any age, though in every age it is on the way. But the divinisation of the world, a Christian culture, a Catholic humanism, are aspirations which we need and which the religious man cannot live without. They are no mere ideologies which are impossible of realisation, like the 'perfect State' of the future, which cannot ever come into being because there is a contradiction in the very idea of it and in its relations with human nature; they are ideals, which are free of any con-tradiction, but which can never be brought to fulfilment in finite time, for the sole reason that they are unlimited, whereas

12

the material on which they depend for their realisation can only offer limited resources of energy.

THE SAINT OF OUR TIMES

The two forms of the religious life, which we have been outlining, have always played an important part in the kingdom of God, along with all their various intermediate forms; nevertheless, the temper of the times and the vital needs of the Church in any given age will lend now the one form, now the other, a heightened significance. When one or the other form becomes predominant, it calls forth the restraining and correcting influence of the other, and even in the case of the individual man, the two forms must be always kept in a state of equilibrium, so that on the one hand activism may not degenerate into a spirit of worldliness and on the other hand mysticism may not sour into hatred for the world, both positions being equally harmful to the kingdom of God. Therefore, when we speak of the saint of our times, we do not wish to imply that he is the only type that is to be recognised or tolerated by our time, or that he was unknown to former ages; all we are saying is that our modern age is particularly congenial to this type and has a special need of him.

The saint in this world

The activistic type represents the union of interior piety and a humanism which is in sympathy with the world, of a spirit of intimate intercourse with God and an enthusiastic spirit of action and decision. He walks in Heaven and on earth at the same time; he sees the heavens opening and the angels of God ascending and descending on men. The hermit, who has cut himself off from the world, nevertheless rejoices in a world which is being transformed ever more from a wilderness into a happy dwelling-place for men, and without feeling any desire to participate directly in this world he can by his prayers and sacrifices effectively support and make fruitful the efforts and struggles of those who are in the world.

In the same way, the man who is cooperating with the

Creator in the formation of a Christian culture, rejoices that there are those who have forsaken the affairs of the world to perfect the divine image in their souls, and he is elated by the feeling that their ultimate purpose is the same as his, even though this vocation of renunciation of the world does not correspond to his own personal dispositions. and though he realises that he can benefit only indirectly from the streams of grace radiated by these brethren of his, whose lives are spent in the direct service of God and are a constant reminder to him of the one thing which is necessary. For the man who spends himself in serving the world, also, the kingdom of God comes first. In the things of the world and in men he sees God, and from God there falls, in turn, a light which illuminates the world and all mankind. The activist can win through to a correct attitude to the world only when he has first learnt to see God properly. Before he came to this true knowledge, the world, as seen by him, was not the real world but only its external appearance, and the life, which he lived, was not really living but vegetating. This, no doubt, explains why Jesus first forgave the sins of the paralytic and gave him a spiritual vision before curing his bodily infirmities.

If we take the expression 'man of the world' in its best sense, we may define the saint of our times as the sanctified man of the world. For such a man, Christianity is not something which stands outside of life, independent and isolated, nor is life something which stands outside of Christianity; for him, rather, life is Christianity and Christianity is life. The idea of the union of Christianity and a noble humanism was a familiar one to the Middle Ages; it has become a problem for us only since the Reformation destroyed this unity and forced its two poles into a relation of friction and antagonism. It is only rarely in modern times that we find the need for this unity expressed. One who does express it is St. Francis de Sales, who realises 'that every noble impulse of human nature can and must be united with the religious aspirations of the Christian.' The great importance of St. Francis de Sales for the development of Christian piety lies in the fact that 'he outlined in his "Introduction to the devout life", the feasibility of a union between the ideal of pure and noble humanity, which was at the heart of the movement of humanism, and the ideal of supernatural man, which Christianity had always preached, and gave in his own life a practical illustration of his theories.'[21] For this reason he has been rightly called by H. Bremond 'the master of devout humanism.'[22] It is a pity that the Saint, influenced by his mystically inclined pupil, St. Jane Frances de Chantal, and by Archbishop de Marquemont of Lyons, allowed himself to be diverted from his original intention of placing the Order of the Visitation, founded by him, at the immediate service of the Christian Renaissance.[23]

The saint in this world is the fulfilment of our true human nature, the realisation of the eternal idea of man in the mind of God; he cooperated in the work of God in the world, and enjoys a more profound knowledge of the world and of men, seeing them as he does from a divine standpoint; he is quick to see the revelation of God in all things and in all experiences, sensitive to the gentle whispers of divine inspiration in his soul and alert for any opportunities to promote God's interests; he possesses a higher freedom, which springs from his participation in the divine nature and which ensures that God's will is always his will. 'Where the Spirit of the Lord is, there is freedom.'[24] The saint can, of course, be pained by his own shortcomings and by the knowledge of how far the reality falls short of the idea of the kingdom of God, and, in fact, he cannot but suffer in seeing these things; yet they only serve to spur him on to do his utmost to narrow the gap which separates him from the ideal.

He scarcely feels the natural law to be in any degree a burden, since it has become a part of his nature, and while in the matter of external freedom something may be left to be desired, he continues to enjoy his interior freedom to the full; meanwhile, he looks forward to the realisation of this exterior freedom, as soon as men and he himself are ready for it. He feels himself to be a part of the Nature which surrounds him, and he sees it not as something indifferent or hostile to God but as the work of the Father and a wonderful manifestation of his grandeur. The history of mankind and of nations and of his own soul is not for him a recital of error and of sin, but rather the finger of God's Providence. In spite of the evils consequent upon original sin, the burden of which he feels weighing upon him also, he

[21] M. Müller, *Die Freundschaft des hl. Franz von Sales mit der hl. Johanna Franziska von Chantal,* Munich 1923, Kosel and Pustet, p. 131.
[22] Cf. Henri Bremond, *Histoire littéraire du sentiment religieux en France* XI, Paris 1924, Librairie Bloud and Gay, pp. 68–127.
[23] Müller, loc. cit., p. 215; [24] 2 Corinthians 3, 17.

respects and honours his body as a companion given him by God and destined for glory, rather than as a prison or an adversary of his soul. Instead of fleeing from men, he feels united to all men as fellow-citizens of the kingdom of God on earth; instead of abandoning the world to the devil, he firmly and inevitably believes in the divinisation of the world, this being the sole purpose for which the world was intended by its Creator. He uses the gifts of Nature with gratitude and enjoys the fruits of the creative spirit, even helping to create them where it is in his power to do so ; but he never allows himself to forget for a single instant, and here he differs from the culture-loving Greek and his German imitators of the Enlightenment, humanist and the Romantic movement, that he cannot and must not indulge in the complacent enjoyment of these things, without being untrue to God and to his own nature, since he is not the owner, but the administrator of the goods of the earth, and since his main task is to cooperate in planting the kingdom of God on earth.

The saint in the world re-introduces a model of sanctity to this earth, from which it had fled or rather, like Astrea, been banished because the men of this earth no longer believed in it or had any use for it. The modern ideal of sanctity is like the sacred fire of Nehemias, which was hidden for so long in the dry cistern, and which is now being inflamed anew by God's sun. In the light of this ideal, old concepts which for many had become insubstantial shadows, have taken on new power and splendour. The idea that the Christian must be a second Christ, and that the individual man must be a child of God, in whom the image of the only-begotten Son of God is to be formed,[25] is meeting with a fresh understanding. These concepts have always been understood by the mystic, but to-day they are becoming familiar to the man in the world and they are such that he can readily recognise their application to his own life. Sanctity, the kingdom of God, Heaven, eternal life are no longer merely eschatological concepts, with no bearing upon this life. To be holy and to attain to eternal life is a charge imposed upon every man, and it is one which is possible, and furthermore obligatory for all men.

In early Christian times, all these ideas were living and ever-present realities: 'the gift of God is life everlasting',[26] and 'he who believes has life everlasting.'[27] The early Christians were not the slightest bit ashamed to call one another 'holy' and

[25] Galatians 4, 19; [26] Romans 6, 23; [27] John 3, 26.

'spiritual'. Eternal life, the kingdom of Heaven and the Communion of Saints are spoken of as things which are close at hand and vividly understood, and while they are not perfectly realised as yet, they have been established and we have received a pledge of them, as it were, in the Holy Spirit of God.

These ideas, so vital when the world impatiently awaited the Second Coming, must be revived to-day, when men are coming to realise that it is their God-given mission to make the present era conform to the image of it in the mind of God. The Church, as the society of men who feel in this way, would not be a castle hidden behind its battlements but rather an open city on a mountain peak to which all would have admittance; it would no longer be just one creed amongst so many, but would be the Catholic community *par excellence* to which, by nature, by law and by the divine will, all that is human must belong. It is only heresy that needs to defend itself and to put itself in a state of siege behind battlements, not, however the Church: 'He, that is not against you is for you.'[28]

The saint has no need to disavow nor to suppress his nature, that is, his humanity. Grace does not destroy nature, at least in its more elevated functions; it does not reduce the saint to a 'scheme'. There is no fixed type, who forms the most suitable subject for sanctity. The saint, as a saint, preserves his own temperament, his passions, his gifts, his inclinations. The only thing is that the saint tries to extirpate from his nature anything which is less noble, that is to say, anything which is contrary to his own better nature and to the divine plan, and which would obstruct the operation of grace. There is nothing extraordinary in the supernatural sense about the saint; the only thing which is extraordinary about him is his fidelity to his vocation and his steadfast love for God and men. 'Communia non communiter', to do the ordinary things in an extraordinary way, is, for St. Bernard, the sum of Christian perfection. And for St. Paul, the way to holiness is through the practice of the virtues proper to one's station in life, that is to say, for the man sobriety, self-control and faithful care of his family, for the woman loving care of those who belong to her household, charity towards the stranger and the fulfilment of her maternal duties.[29]

The religious ideal is not something which runs parallel to the moral ideal, rather it includes it. The more one is prepared

[28] Mark 9, 39; [29] 1 Timothy 2, 8–15; 5, 8 10 14; Titus 2, 2–6 and several other texts.

for the reception of grace, the more will grace be able to reveal its true powers. According as grace takes possession of man, it illuminates the moral values and all the other values for him. Nature must become so ennobled that it can pursue its way and exercise its vital energies without ever coming into conflict with religion; it must even reach the stage where it can be certain in advance that it will do and wish to do only that which is in accordance with God's will. The saint, as we are describing him here, might well adopt for his motto the words of St. Augustine: 'Love God and do as you will.' His model is not the Indian Yogi, who is insensible to all worldly needs or calls, but the man of inner harmony, in whom body and soul, nature and culture, religion and life form an intrinsic unity; it is not the Encratite, who looks upon the soul and the intellect with a jaundiced eye, but the man who is master of himself and enjoys complete interior freedom, and who is so much above the things of this world that he can take them or leave them alone.

Looking at it, then, from this perspective, the idea of the saint which has been current for so long requires to be corrected. This pictures the saint as a being without flesh and blood, without any past history or interior progression in holiness, without struggles or problems, in short, a man out of another world. And this false picture of sanctity has been fostered for so long, by the way in which the lives of the saints were written, thus hindering the development of a healthy asceticism. There have, of course, been saints, who were indifferent to the demands of worldly culture. This is very easy to understand, as men, whose souls were full of the knowledge of God and of divine energy, could not feel themselves enriched by worldly goods, which in fact only distracted them from the clear vision and the intimate possession of higher things. But they were not saints merely because they were indifferent to earthly values, but rather in spite of it. Yet amongst the men of great spirituality in every age, and particularly amongst the saints of the Church, there have been men of superior intellectual culture and the most refined nobility of soul. It would be very difficult to name a humanist, even the most noble, to surpass a Francis de Sales, a Fenélon or a Newman, considered as men of culture. In the saint and the Christian destined for sanctity, the child of God and the man are united in the one person. The pagan humanist and the Christian saint are very close to one another in their outward appearances, and, in fact, when both are

present in their most ideal form, they can scarcely be distinguished outwardly; yet, there is an infinite distance between
them both in their value and in their actual being. They are
as near to each other and yet as far apart for the mathematician,
as two tangents projected to infinity, the one positive and the
other negative.

Jesus himself, in his life and in his teaching, is the model of
the most noble humanism. He is the most noble, the wisest,
the purest, the freest and the most beautiful of all men. Jesus
is no extreme ascetic turning away in distaste from the world.
He contrasts the Son of Man, who eats and drinks, even at the
risk of being branded as a glutton and a drunkard, with the
Baptist, who neither ate nor drank and who was therefore
reviled as one having a devil.[30] Yet how much more sweetly
the glad tidings of Jesus fall on our ears compared to the stern
message of repentance brought by John! How easily and without
restraint he takes part in the life of the people! He does not
despise the marks of deference and honour which are customary
in social intercourse, and is conscious of the slight, when these
marks of honour are witheld from him.[31] He takes part with
simple composure in banquets arranged in his honour,[32]
and even manifests a certain enjoyment of them.[33] He does
not wear a penitential robe nor an ascetic garment, as did his
Precursor, nor does he go in beggar's rags,[34] but rather con-
forms in the matter of dress to the accepted practice amongst
Jewish teachers.[35] He does not insist that his disciples fast,
because one cannot expect the wedding-guests to fast while
the bridegroom is still with them.[36] He instructs his mission-
aries to eat and drink what is put before them, for the labourer
is worthy of his hire; even, however, in the matter of eating
and drinking, the messengers of the Lord must show their
interior liberty and their self-mastery.[37]

Jesus is in sympathy with human nature and enjoys the
company of good people. He converses with publicans and
sinners, with those who are athirst for salvation and those
who do not feel this thirst at all. His parables draw freely and
easily upon images from Nature, and also from such things as
banquets and weddings. His teaching, particularly in his
parables, is of unrivalled simplicity and irresistible beauty,
and reveals a richness of thought which is inexhaustible. He

[30] Matthew 11, 18 f.; [31] Luke 7, 44–46; [32] Luke 5, 29; 19, 6; John 12,2,
[33] Luke 7, 37 f.; [34] Matthew 27, 31, and John 19, 23; [35] John 4, 11;
[36] Mark 2, 18 f.; [37] Luke 10, 7 f.

rejoices with the happy and weeps with the sad. Nor is he merely a cosmopolitan reformer of humanity, but loves his home town and his country, and has a keen eye for the beauties of his native landscape, for the birds of the air and the lilies of the fields. He is sensitive to honest love and friendship. He allows himself to be conducted into Jerusalem in triumph. Amongst the many factors, which distinguish him from most other religious reformers, and particularly from Buddha, is his fidelity to nature. He is an activist in the noblest sense of the word, in spite of his constant and uninterrupted communion with the Father. He is a worker, as is his Father.[38] The words 'work' and 'activity' play an important and ever-recurring role in his teaching. And St. Paul speaks sharply of those teachers of error, who: 'Forbidding to marry, to abstain from meats, which God hath created to be received with thanksgiving by the faithful and by them that have known the truth. For every creature of God is good, and nothing to be rejected that is received with thanksgiving.'[39]

On the other hand, it is equally easy to adduce abundant proof that Jesus wishes us to despise the present world, that he warns us of it, and that he tells us to deny ourselves and take up the cross, if we are to follow him. Especially from those who are to be the leaders in his kingdom, he demands not only an interior but also an exterior separation from father and mother, brother and sister, house and lands. Not all, however, are called, as was the rich young man, to leave behind all their possessions. This call is only for those who wish to be his intimate companions. He holds friendly intercourse with men and families from whom he does not expect such a sacrifice. At the same time, a man, for whom God and the kingdom of God is everything, cannot so identify himself with the interests of the world that he is content to dwell on them entirely. The disciple of Jesus, especially if he wishes to be a leader in his kingdom, must freely renounce many values, in order to devote himself more completely to his calling. However, it is not this leader alone who is warned not to become over-attached to the world, for 'if any man love the world, the charity of the Father is not in him';[40] likewise for the man who devotes himself to serving the world, the world must not be his ultimate goal, nor even the ennoblement of the world by imprinting on it the image of God and of the perfect man; his ultimate goal must

[38] John 5, 17; [39] Timothy 4, 3 f.; cf. Colossians 2, 20–23.
[40] 1 John 2, 15.

be God alone. Here again, we are brought face to face with the two different concepts of the world: the world as evil and opposed to God, which we must avoid; and the world, which is to be transfigured and glorified by means of our cooperation.

The roots of all true culture and prosperity can be found in the message brought to us by Jesus about our divine filiation, for if men are really children of God, then they are also noble. If men could come to regard themselves as members of one divine family and as brothers and sisters in Christ, then the social problem would be solved, at least in its broad outlines. Then we could truly say that the kingdom of God was come amongst us.

The ideal saint of today

The saint in this world proceeds from this sublime principle: Vocation is the same as the service of God. Assuming that it is made freely and after due consideration of all the external and internal circumstances, the choice of any honest calling is confirmed by God, and is the calling of that particular man to God. The man, who is thus called, can now say: God, who governs all the events of human life, has assigned to me this place in human society; it is in his name and by his will that I am acting here, and all that I do is done in his service. Such a man will never feel discontented with his calling.[41] For the man in the world who is pursuing sanctification, work and prayer are only two different aspects of one and the same divine worship; he is not worried about snatching off every available moment from work to give himself to prayer; he realises that work or rest or enjoyment, when willed by God, is itself prayer. Similarly, he does not regard the time devoted to prayer as unproductive, as the purely humanistic man would, since he realises that prayer is the noblest possible spiritual activity. He ignores that lamentable distinction, which others make, between prayer as a spontaneous effusion of piety and prayer as a duty.

Nor must we think that this religious approach to the world and its goods, will make the soul indifferent to such things as human love and friendship: on the contrary! In God all relationships are set on a firm foundation and seen in their true light, and he is the ultimate principle and supreme guarantee of all

[41] 1 Corinthians 7, 20.

true love and loyal friendship. The 'wise man' in Ecclesiasticus
and the 'valiant woman' in the Book of Proverbs are concrete
representations of the harmonious union of fidelity to God
and fidelity to the world, one's nation, one's family, one's
calling. The divine mandate given in Paradise is heard again in
the demands of the most noble part of our nature, which tells
us that work is the finest and noblest service of God, and that
the service of God is the highest form of activity.

There is also such a thing as primitive sanctity. The primitive
saint lives without reflection, just like the child, who lives
without being aware of it, or the healthy man, who breathes
without paying attention to it or whose heart beats without
his feeling it; or like man in the state of Paradise, who did not
know good and evil. This form of sanctity, however, is enjoyed
by very few. Once we have sinned, or at least come to know the
necessity for struggling against sin, we can no longer live in a
state of naïve ingenuousness, but need reflection to assure
ourselves that there is agreement between what we are and what
we ought to be. The more, however, a unity between religion
and life is restored, the more the religious man will return to
the natural goodness of the child, and the less need he will have
for reflection or for consciously referring his actions to God.
He has no need of different formulas and techniques for awakening purity of intention, because his whole life, and hence
each individual act, is imbued with this purity of intention.

'Separate acts of faith are important for us', says Cardinal
Newman,[42] 'only as long as we are not confirmed in the faith;
once firmly grounded in faith, however, our whole life becomes,
as it were, a single continuous act of faith, just as our day's
work becomes one single act of obedience.' Hence when a man
really lives by faith, his whole life is a continuous service of
God. 'The mass of men see God at a distance; and when they
try to be religious, they strain their eyes towards this distant
light, and grope their way. The Christian, however, who is
well-versed and experienced in the practice of his faith, who
has succeeded in coming closer to God by means of his grace,
the elect of God, in whom dwells the Holy Spirit, he has no
need to strain his eyes to discern the footprints of the Master,
but allows himself to be guided by the indwelling Holy Spirit.
When he follows his interior impulses, he knows himself to be
on the right track.' Newman hastens to add, however: 'I do
not say that there is any man, who actually lives in this way,

---

[42] Przywara-Karrer, *J. H. Newman* in *Christentum*, VIII, 41 ff.

for this kind of life is proper to the angels. But it is the spiritual state, towards which the zealous Christian must aspire and endeavour to approach by obeying the divine command to "watch and pray".'

This way of looking at life neither gives rise to a languid passivity, as if God alone could be depended on to do everything by himself, nor to an over-eager activity, as if nothing could be done except by human powers. Similarly, it steers a middle course between that self-confidence which would make all success dependent on human effort, and that excessive confidence in God, which would make all human effort vain. For the saint of the activistic life, self-confidence and confidence in God are fused together to form the one confidence, a confidence in our own human powers, which have been bestowed by God and which, when used in accordance with his will, will be rewarded with success. Men of this type throw themselves with irresistible ardour into the struggle for the kingdom of God, yet at the same time, they entrust everything to the hands of God, who lets the cockle grow along with the wheat until the time of the harvest; they enjoy that happy, trusting state of soul, which never permits them to despair of God, of themselves, or of the people, of the Church, of humanity, and which allows them to hope even when all hope seems lost, because in all their activities they see the hand of God at work and they realise that they are helping him to achieve his purposes.

This optimism has no need to take refuge in illusions to evade the harsh realities of life; it is not that overweening confidence in life, which springs from the instinct of self-preservation, nor that optimism, which springs from a spiritual nostalgia for a kingdom, in which all will be perfectly true, good and beautiful, nor is it that optimism, which forces itself to a heroic confidence in a logical purpose of existence, [43] and hence never comes to anything more than a rational optimism. It is rather an optimism, which is based on faith in a divine order governing the world; and the Christian acquiesces cheerfully and lovingly in this order, since he sees God not merely as a metaphysical explanation for the existence of the world and the guide of its destinies, but also as a God of grace and salvation, who has given to the creatures of his love a share in his own life. This optimism gives rise to the strongest motives for consecrating oneself to promoting secular values, since these belong at the

[43] Thus Hans Rosenfeld, *Glaube und Weltanschauung*, Berlin 1928, Lambert Schneider.

same time to the kingdom of God, the coming of which depends upon the work of men.

For the Christian optimist, religion is not a kind of fetish, which is carried into the field of battle and, when the troops waver and begin to retreat, packed away and carried off by the captain to a place of safety. This optimist is the standard-bearer of progress in everything which relates to the true, the good and the beautiful; he is nurtured by the confidence, which the prophet Isaias gives voice to in the words: 'So shall my world be, which shall go forth from my mouth: It shall not return to me void, but it shall do whatsoever I please and shall prosper in the things for which I sent it.'[44]

The physical resources of the active Christian are not increased by this spirit of confidence and optimism, but he learns to husband them with thrift and to utilise them to the best possible advantage, since he feels a sense of responsibility for the capital of bodily and spiritual resources, which is lent to him to be invested towards the fulfilment of God's sacred purposes. Even the greatest disappointments and disillusion-ments which he has to suffer in his dealings with men cannot shake this optimism; on the contrary, the greater the disasters of life seem to be, the stronger grows his trust in God; the more he seems to be forsaken by God, the more trustingly he commits his soul into the hands of God, his eternal Father.

This approach to life is at once mild and stern. The most supreme freedom is at the same time the most powerful re-straint, for the true interior freedom which binds a man to God is ten times stronger than any mere external legalistic bond. It gives rise to a tireless activity united to a perfect peace of soul and security; a constant feeling of fulfilment together with an insatiable desire; waiting impatiently for the coming of the kingdom of God in the world while possessing it already in the silence of the heart; constant equilibrium along with an ever-active tension; a joyous approval of life as it is, together with a sacred seriousness and concern for life and for oneself, which does not permit one to enjoy much pleasure but nevertheless brings in its wake a profound joy and peace.

This state of soul is beyond the comprehension of many people. Some cannot understand how he can be so much in love with the world, which is hated and feared by them; in fact, he often loves it so much that he has to withdraw from a place of suffering lest he irritate others, who cannot understand

[44] Isaias 55, 11.

or appreciate his joyous serenity in the face of this sorrow; others who are dragged under by worldly desires cannot understand how he can love the world without becoming worldly-minded. Some take him to task for being too carefree, for not being sensible to human misery, for not bewailing the past more bitterly and doing penance for his faults, for not showing more energy in scourging vice and pillorying injustice; while others despise him as an austere prig, who cannot relax and enjoy the pleasures of life, but must be always finding some new task which has to be carried out. And we must remember that even Jesus was not forgiven for being the friend of publicans and sinners[45] and for refusing to throw the first stone at the woman taken in adultery.[46]

He who has placed all his hopes in God can expect but little from the rest of mankind. The greatest and most far-reaching decisions above all, can have the effect of putting him in a place of solitude apart, where he is separated from the rest of the world by an unbridgeable chasm. Jesus, for instance, was so far removed from the comprehension of men that his followers thought for a time, that he was mad,[47] and even as a twelve-year-old in the Temple, his parents could not understand him.[48] This realm of spiritual solitude and isolation may have a superficial resemblance to the 'polar wastes', in which Nietzsche places the soul which is homeless and far from God; in reality, it is a solitude in which one is alone with God, and hence, a communion of the greatest intimacy and warmth. Hence the goal of the religious man who is devoted to the world must always remain in the realm of the ideal, by which we mean that, since the end of all possible development is to be a 'second Christ' and yet one can never be another Christ, it is impossible to be a perfect Christian. Yet this is the goal at which we must aim. We can never overtake the first Christ, but we must follow him as far as we can along the way.

Without this ideal we cannot act or even live. Thus it is that our activism must always have a note of incompletion ; it is a strange paradox that we must be always on the move like the wandering Jew and yet never arrive at our goal. Hence in the depths of his spirit, the religious man feels a constant dissatisfaction, which is in proportion to the clarity with which he sees the goal and the intensity with which he pursues it.

[45] Matthew 11, 19; [46] John 8, 7; [47] Mark 3, 21.
[48] Luke 2, 50.

He cries out with Thomas a' Kempis,[49] 'How the earth chafes
upon me, when I think of Heaven', for 'whatever is not God
is nothing, where the satisfaction of our spirit is concerned, and
must be accounted as nothing.' And Friedrich Naumann says,
'A Christian, who is nothing else but a Christian, is not possible
in this world, . . . for Christianity is not the whole of life, but
one dimension of it.'[50] Thus our weariness of earth and our
nostalgia for Heaven continue to cause us pain, but at the same
time they give the soul strength to carry on the struggle. When
a man works for the kingdom of God in himself and in the world
around him, he realises the truth of St. Paul's words about
'sowing in tears', and this holds not only for the mystic but also
for the activist. The latter, in fact, feels more keenly than other
men the decadence of humanity and of himself, and is pained
by what he sees of the state of humanity, the State, the people,
the Church, and most of all, of himself; yet he believes in the
possibility of a better future for man in society, in marriage,
in the State, in the Church, and believes moreover that this
better future will one day be realised. He is pained by the way
in which men are divided into different religious creeds and
sects but looks forward with confidence to the day when people
of all races and all tongues will be gathered together in the unity
of the faith.

The world of to-day calls for a new saint who will take his
place beside the old revered figures of our history and legend,
for the sanctified 'man of the world', the man, who will form
all the various aspects of humanity in order of value into a
harmonious union and will join this integral humanity with a
lively faith in God, an ardent love of him and a self-sacrificing
willingness to be assimilated into the life of his Church. It is
true that the perfect harmony of these elements is something
which is beyond the reach of the individual and of society;
only one man has ever completely realised this idea, Jesus
Christ, the Son of God and the Son of Man. He is, therefore,
our model for all times, and it is only by following him that
we can arrive at a state of noble humanism. Every Christian can
and must follow him, and thus approach as near to noble
humanity and to sanctity as it is given to him to approach.

It is only by such ideals that we can live! It is not the goal
which is easy of attainment but the goal which is infinite that
has most power to attract the human soul with its innate

---

[49] Imitation of Christ, 3: 31.
[50] *Briefe über Religion*,[17] Berlin 1916, Georg Reimer, p. 74 f.

tendency to seek the supreme good. The saint is never able to rest content with what has been already achieved. He knows that the kingdom of God is always coming, but is never fully realised; it is only in a life beyond time that the kingdom of God will become a reality in all its perfection. But since God accepts the will to act rather than the actual deed and since every movement takes its name and its value from the goal towards which it is directed, it follows that, even here in this life, we must have the saint in the office, the saint in business, industry and politics, the saint in the professor's chair, at the workmen's bench and behind the plough, we must have sanctity both in the lowly housewife and in the lady of rank and fashion. The saint in this world must cooperate in the establishment of the new family, the new State, the new society, the new humanity, the new creation, the new kingdom of God. May the good God still the longings of our age by giving it many such saints!